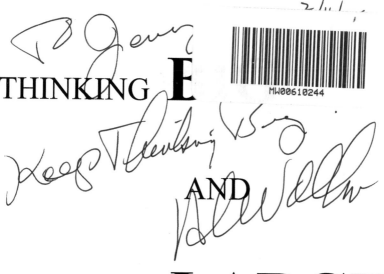

THINKING E

AND

LIVING LARGE

OR

LITTLE LIVING IS FOR THE SMALL MINDED

And who should know better than

Al Walker

Professional Speaker & Author

Printed in the United States of America
10 9 8 7 6 5 4 3

Cataloging in Publication Data

Walker, E. Albert
 Thinking Big and Living Large/Al Walker

ISBN Number: 1-59196-375-3

For information contact:

Al Walker
PO Box 542
Chapin, SC 29036
(803) 345-1050
al@alwalker.com
www.alwalker.com

DEDICATION

This book is dedicated to my best buddy, Robert Henry, CSP, CPAE, Cavett Award Winner, Past President of the National Speakers Association, and one of the greatest encouragers on the planet. He probably helped more aspiring speakers than anyone else I have ever known.

Robert passed away in September of 2001 after complications from diabetes and a bout with cancer. He fought a hard fight, kept his sense of humor up to the very end, and was an outstanding witness to his faith in God and how to think big and live large. He lived, loved, and laughed every single day that I knew him for over twenty years.

Hanging on the wall over my desk is a large framed photo of Robert and it is signed with these words that Robert wrote on the bottom of the picture:

To Al Walker
- My most wonderful and dearest friend.

Robert H. Henry.

This book is dedicated to you, my friend. If it brings one tenth of the laughter and love for life that you shared with all of us, it just might change the world...

FORWARD

By

Margaret Walker

Most people wait their entire lies for something BIG to happen to them. Well, something *really* BIG happened to me a few years ago. I met Al Walker on a blind date, and with his beautiful and generous spirit, he made me love him. I didn't want to do it...Noooo, I didn't want to do it (hmmm...does anyone else hear a song?)! Before I knew it, in fact, in just two months, I married him. As you might imagine, even though I thought I knew what I was doing, I really did not know him very well when we married. I had never heard of an organization called the National Speakers Association, let alone that Al had been the past-president. In fact, I had never even heard him speak (professionally); so, naturally I did not understand the professional letters and designations that came after his name and what they represented – CSP, CPAE, a member of the prestigious Platform Professionals (which means he is linked to such speaking greats as Jeanne Robertson, Doc Blakely, Bryan Townsend, Lou Heckler, and Charles Petty), and a Cavett Award winner! I almost hate to admit this, but at the first NSA convention that I attended, I was disappointed to learn that Dick Cavett was not even a member! After being duly informed, I was fortunate enough to meet <u>The</u> Cavett – Cavett Robert, that is – and his lovely wife, Miss Trudy. When I learned that Miss Trudy was a former Miss South Carolina...well, now we're talking about "home folks!" *That* is familiar territory, and I knew I was in good company.

Now, as well known as Al Walker might be, there are some things you may not know about him. He works tirelessly for speakers and the National Speakers Association (NSA). Although he has commanded every office, held just about every position, and won every award in the NSA, Al continues to work behind the scenes in whatever capacity is needed. He has been the chair of the Foundation

4

Board of Governors. He sits on boards of educational institutions, charities, and is a deacon, choir member and leader in our home church – St. Andrews Baptist. In addition to the time, energy, and resources he spends on his faith, his family, his friends, his community, his country, and the efforts he exerts to make this world a better place…he still finds the time to make me feel like I am the center of his world! That takes a really BIG man – a great man – generous almost to a fault…a giver of gifts, not the least of which is himself…he gives his "all," not only to me, but to many. I fell in love with something really BIG – a man with strong values, vision and veracity. If you are not familiar with AL WALKER, then you, too, are about to embark on a blind date full of the wit, wisdom, insight, and even some of the mischief that is just liable to have you falling in love (well, maybe you'll just trip). As you absorb his words, prepare yourself to take to heart his message of laughter and love…because I'm tellin' you…something *really* BIG is getting ready to take place…right here…for you.

I should know.
It happened to me.

5

A BOOK ABOUT LIVING A LARGE LIFE TO THE FULLEST

Preface

This book is about *thinking* **BIG**, not about *being* **BIG**. If you are truly tired of little living and want to live a **BIGGER**, fuller, richer life, then this book is for you. What are the possibilities, when a person really does think creatively and moves away from the familiar things that have kept them where they are into the unknown? Can we ever think **BIG** enough and, if we do, will be guaranteed a **LARGER** life? Yes! Even if we don't fulfill our dreams, I know beyond any shadow of a doubt that our lives will be richer, deeper and better just because we tried.

I'm convinced, beyond any shadow of a doubt, that God put a lot of potential in each of us and that he expects us to use it to the fullest. My prayer is that the words on these pages will inspire you to tap more deeply into the talents, skills and abilities God has given you so that you can live the life he intended you to live.

Just a few short years ago, it dawned on me that I have spent most of my adult life around **Big** time winners. Not that I went out seeking them, I just ended up being with them because of my work. Now I hunt them down and do my best to learn everything I can from and about them.

As a Professional Speaker, I have had the honor of being with the cream of the crop from all walks of life. Almost every place I speak I am surrounded by people who are either winning Big awards, have achieved some Big goal or are the people who are at a conference or convention to learn something new. Some have been celebrities, yet most have not been famous. At least, not famous to the general public, but they were and are standouts in their own organization or profession. They are admired and respected by their peers as much as "celebrities" are by the general public.

As I've heard them tell their stories over the years, I've realized they all share some common traits, characteristics, and values. I've been sharing what I've learned from them in as humorous, as entertaining, and hopefully, as inspiring a way as I know how and I've been doing it for over twenty years.

That is what this book is about. It is full of the winning commonalities I've seen in individuals or organizations that any one of us would label as being successful and the stories I tell to illustrate those characteristics. All in the hope of passing as much of the winning mental DNA on to as many folks as I possibly could. That's also the reason I've written this book. If one person has a better life and comes even just a little closer to achieving his or her capabilities, then all the speeches, all the time spent researching, and all the hours spent writing this will have certainly been worthwhile.

One thing you will notice as you read through these pages is that a lot of the people I mention faced the same challenges the rest of us face. They just deal with them a little differently than most people. They are somehow able to handle the difficulties of life in a **BIGGER,** more enriching way. This book tells you exactly what you need to do to make any particular trait, characteristic, or value a part of your life and how you can include it in your plan to live a **LARGER** life.

People who know me or have seen me in audiences from Anaheim to Annapolis and from San Juan to Seattle might be thinking I'm going to write about how to be over six feet tall and weigh over 350 pounds, since that describes the size I've been most of my adult life. As exciting reading as that would be (he says with tongue in cheek), that is not the purpose of this book. Maybe I'll let that be my next book and I'll tell you all about my favorite foods, how exercise will kill you, and how energizing it can be to relax for 3 hours in a hammock, read a book, and then take a nap.

This book is for everybody. It is full of the stories and illustrations I've been using in my talks for these more than twenty five years. Even if you've "made it," there will be something in these pages that just might challenge you to think even **BIGGER** and live even **LARGER**.

7

One of the richest people in the USA in the 20th century was a man named J. Paul Getty and it was reported that he was once asked, "How much is enough"? His reply was, "Just a little bit more." So no matter how **BIG** your **THINKING** or how **LARGE** your **LIVING** is today, there's always room for "just a little bit more."

You can decide for yourself how funny or poignant or inspiring these stories, jokes and examples are – my hope is that in reading it, you get a few good laughs along the way and that you enjoy this book to the fullest. I also hope that it encourages, uplifts and challenges you to always be guilty of:

"THINKING BIG AND LIVING LARGE"

CONTENTS

Introduction

BIG PREPARATION

"PLEASE HELP ME WELCOME. . .A BIG MAN WITH A BIG MESSAGE. . .MR. AL WALKER."

That is usually the last line I hear as I'm being introduced to an audience. As I step to the front of the room, I let the audience know fairly quickly that I love to laugh, that I can laugh at myself and that there's a pretty good chance we're going to laugh a lot while we're together. One of my dear speaker friends, Bob Murphy says that if you can get up in the morning, look at yourself in the mirror and laugh at what you see, you're gonna make it.

Folks who can laugh at themselves are probably not only going to make it, but they say to the world they are confident and self-assured. More importantly, they have a real healthy self-esteem, which means their ego is strong.

As a professional speaker, the funny stuff usually starts the minute we are on site and I meet the meeting planner or leaders in the organization for the first time. That occurs most of the time when I walk into a room that has been set up for a meal. I am especially amused over the years at some of the questions people have asked me during those times as we sat together at a breakfast, luncheon, or dinner banquet table. Some of their questions have been interesting, while some are down right funny. There are two questions I get asked more than any other. One is, "Do you still get nervous before you speak?" and the other is, "Do you always eat before you speak?"

That second question usually comes as I'm stuffing a bite of cheese cake in my mouth. My answer to the first question is usually, "No, I don't get nervous like I did when I first started, but I do try to pump myself up before I speak so I can get some adrenalin running through my veins." That usually satisfies them, however on a few rare occasions some have asked, "How do you do that?" I then go on to tell them there are two things I do before every talk.

The first is I give myself a pep talk that is very specific. It consists of three parts. Part one is I tell myself this is going to be the greatest talk I've ever given and that it is the most *important* talk I've ever given. Several years ago I genuinely convinced myself of two significant concepts. The first is that I can't go back and relive any talk, no matter how much I might want to. Plus, there is not a single word in any talk I have already given that I could go back and change. The second concept is that no matter how many talks I might have scheduled on the calendar in the months and years ahead, I might not make it to the next one, so the talk I'm about to give is the most important one of all, whether it is to a group of ten people at an office park in my home town of Columbia, South Carolina or to several thousand people in Las Vegas, Nevada.

In Part two of my pep talk, I mentally go over the three or four reasons why I think this particular talk is going to be successful. I'll repeat such thoughts as: "I've been doing this successfully for over 20 years. I've had standing ovations from most of my audiences, the majority of whom have recommended me to others and have brought me back for repeat engagements. I've been recognized by my peers who have told me I'm one of the very best professional speakers on the platform today." Those kinds of thoughts are very reinforcing to me. They remind me of the success I've had, and since I believe past performance is a pretty good indicator of future performance, this *will* be one of the best talks I've ever given.

In part three, I go over a few of the benefits that might come my way, if I do an outstanding job such as: "I'll have a happy meeting planner; the audience will feel their time has been well spent; someone in the audience will go through a life changing experience or, at least, be stimulated enough to make some needed changes in their life; I'll continue to build my reputation as a professional speaker and I'll either get more speaking engagements from audience members or this group will want me back or better yet, both."

Then I follow that with a short prayer for my audience and me. Then I repeat ..."Let the words of my mouth and the meditations of my heart be acceptable in Thy sight, oh Lord, my strength and my redeemer."

When I use both the Pep Talk and the Prayer before I give a speech, I seem to 1. Get in the right frame of mind and 2. Get more excited about giving this talk, to these people at this point in time.

With regard to the second question that is usually asked, as I'm enjoying that bite of cheesecake I told you about earlier when someone asks, if I always eat before I speak, my response is always the same. I stop and with a smile on my face and laughter in my voice say, "Are you serious, I want you to take a closer look at me and ask that question again, if you can do it with a straight face." Then, as they reexamine me, they start to laugh...knowing I didn't get the size I am by missing too many meals, including the ones given me right before I speak. The truth is that I usually eat before I do anything. Just a side note here that I don't usually share - there are a few things I will not eat because they tend to restrict my vocal cords - one is the cheesecake I just mentioned and such stuff as dairy products, icy drinks, and heavy sauces, but almost everything else is fair game.

I want to keep the atmosphere as light and humorous as I can. Anything any of us can do to contribute to that kind of environment always helps everyone else have a better time, no matter where we are. One of the ways I do that is by having an introduction that not only tells the audience who I am, why I'm there, and why I've earned the right to be their speaker, but also to weave in something that makes the introducer look good.

I believe every speaker should have a prepared introduction that fits him or her and their purpose for being wherever they are. As a motivational humorist, I give my introducers a written introduction with a beginning sentence that always gets a laugh - if they deliver it even close to right. Then I end the introduction with another line that has a pretty good chance of arousing another bit of laughter.

If I can give the introducer something to say that gets a laugh, now I have a new friend in the introducer because I've made him or her look good. They sounded prepared, plus they got a couple of good laughs. In the middle of all that they also were able to tell the audience the pertinent things about me that gave me the right to be there. They also gave the audience some reason to listen to me, at least, for the first few minutes. Then, it's up to me to do my part and hold their attention. My introduction also has comments in it about my size that set up an entire section on humor that has served me well for a long time.

When I start speaking, I always try to make the introducer look good by referring to something the introducer said that is a seque into my material. On a few rare occasions, when I knew the situation was right, I got a huge laugh from the audience at the expense of the introducer. For example, one year I spoke at an annual Realtors Association banquet in a major city. It was a formal affair and the ballroom in the hotel was beautifully and festively decorated. When I arrived at the reception prior to the meal, I met the President and his wife. I immediately noticed there was a significant age difference between them of, at least, 25 years. As I met others at the reception and got into conversations with them, I found out that the president had been recently married to this, his third or fourth, wife and that she was very young. It came up a few times in different conversations. Enough times to tell me that everyone was aware of it and the new bride's age was a topic of conversation.

As we sat down at the head table, the president sat to the right of the lectern, facing the audience, his young bride sat next to him and I was seated next to her on her right. I must say she was stunning. She was very fit, very pretty, and very sexy, but not very bright. Sitting there next to her, I realized the dress she had on was very short. It was almost like she was wearing a long tee shirt with sequins that barely covered the top of her legs. You would have stared, too!

This president was not particularly loved by the membership or by the real estate community in general. He was arrogant and very self-absorbed. He was also extremely proud of his trophy bride. As we ate dinner, we chatted about their recent nuptials and also about the significant age difference. I asked if they would mind if I said something about their marriage and, even, if it was ok for me to say something about their age difference in a "pokin' fun" kind of way. They said sure.

The reason I asked is because, as this situation unfolded before me, I recalled a similar situation that had happened in my hometown with an executive of one of our largest employers. I also recalled a comment some of his employees made after his third marriage to a child bride.

So, when I stood up to speak following his introduction, I told the audience how excited I was about being with them and how I had thoroughly enjoyed visiting with their president and his new bride over dinner. I then said, "One of the things we talked about was the age difference and the challenges presented by that. And I want you to know rumor has it that Mr. Jones' next wife hasn't even been born yet."

The place fell apart. The spontaneous eruption of laughter startled me. I knew the line would get a laugh, but I didn't know it would get such loud and explosive laughter. I glanced over at the president and his wife and, thank goodness, they were laughing. I don't believe to this day, they realized what a tremendous shot I had taken at them. It dawned on me later that the reason the laughter was so sudden was because I said what almost everybody else had been thinking, but didn't want to mention publicly. I do not recommend getting your laughs at the introducer's expense, particularly if it makes them look bad, but on this occasion, it worked and it worked BIG.

I've seen that same process manifested in casual conversation, at business meetings, and even when two people are introduced on the street. I know what I want my audience to hear about me. I believe the BIG winners in the world have a way of getting their message about who they are across to everybody they meet, and the real winners do it in an unobtrusive way.

One of the biggest challenges I had early on in my speaking career was feeling like I was tooting my own horn too loud. I felt like my ego was out in front of me more than I wanted it to be and that I was beginning to sound like I believed my own press. Somebody once told me though, "if you don't toot your own horn, it probably won't get tooted," and I gradually began to feel ok with a somewhat self-grandizing introduction. Then I had a major breakthrough and thought to myself that if I wanted people to want to listen to me, I would tell them whatever I needed to tell them that would accomplish that purpose, as long as it was the absolute truth. Then, as someone else once said, "if it's fact, it ain't bragging."

So, I want to encourage you to start with thinking BIG thoughts about yourself, who you really are, what you stand for and believe in. What are your accomplishments and your successes? Be proud of what you've done and keep adding to it. Another someone once told me, "if you don't believe in yourself, that probably makes it unanimous."

When I decided to become a professional speaker, I joined the Association for professional speakers, The National Speakers Association in Tempe, Arizona. When I found out the credentials the top speakers had, I went after them. The only earned designation in NSA is called the CSP or Certified Speaking Professional. I reached that plateau four years after I joined. The next award came just a couple of years later from my peers who only recognize five professional speakers each year. Those five receive The Council of Peers Award for Excellence (CPAE) and are admitted to the Speakers Hall of Fame. Other recipients have included Art Linkletter, Og Mandino, Dr. Norman Vincent Peale, Colin Powell, and Ronald Reagan. Then, a few years later, I was given the most coveted award in NSA. An award given to only one person each year who has, for a number of years, shown the same compassionate sharing and caring attitude so evident in the founder of the National Speakers Association. . .my dear friend and husband to the lovely Mrs. Trudy (the first Miss South Carolina). . . Mr. Cavett Robert. The award is called The Cavett…not the Dick Cavett award, nor the Caveat award, nor the Cravet award, as I've heard it from some of my introducers but THE CAVETT. It is a bronze statue of the man himself – Cavett

Robert in one of his signature poses with his arm stuck straight out in front of him with extended index finger pointing at the audience and it stands proudly in my office today.

The bottom line here is that it took me over ten years to do all that, but I did it because I realized those were the credentials I wanted to combine with the talents God gave me that would put me at the top of my field. What do you need to put you at the top of your field? What recognition, awards and achievements do you need to earn or receive in order to be recognized as one of the very best in your business? Whatever they are, set your course for them today. The pursuit alone will re-energize you.

I honestly believe that if you will read, study, and apply the information in the ten chapters in this book, you will think bigger and have a desire to live larger – not in terms of wealth, or bigger houses, cars or boats, but to experience the fullness of life; to know the joy that comes from challenging yourself to attain new heights – whatever they may be. I wish you the best on your journey and pray that God will bless you as richly as He has blessed me.

Al Walker
Chapin, SC

Chapter 1

BIG VALUES

"Knowing what we stand for and believe in enables us to make the right decision when we don't have time to think about it."

Those with strong values that stand for what is right and good and decent and honorable are more valuable to society than those with values that devalue human life and are participants in the game of life simply for whatever they can get. They want to take short cuts and don't really care who they hurt along the way. Some of them "arrive" only to find themselves all alone and having to leave all they've attained to people who don't even like them. That may not be "news" to you, but it apparently is to a lot of people based on the way they behave and interact with others.

My parents always tried to not only instill the best values in me at home, but they also exposed me to organizations that taught honorable values, such as church, scouting, and DeMolay. My value system was also formed as a result of the experience that comes from applying the wrong values.

Here's an early example that I know contributed to my value system. I was a Cub Scout, a Boy Scout, and an Explorer Scout. When I made the move from Cub Scouts to Boy Scouts, I learned that our scoutmaster spent the majority of his scouting time either planning camping trips or taking us on camping trips. He never put much emphasis on merit badges and rank. That's one of the major reasons we never had one single Eagle Scout from our troop. Looking back, I know there were a few very bright, talented, and skilled members of our troop who could have been Eagle Scouts had they been given the right guidance. A few of us made it to the rank of Star, but that was about it. I guess we spent so much time either camping or getting ready to camp that we never had much time for those other pursuits.

My most memorable scout camping trip was to the Cherokee Indian Reservation in Cherokee, NC, where we were to camp with some other scouts for a week. Cherokee is about 100 miles away from my hometown of Columbia, SC.

Before I tell you about this trip, you need to know that my parents, Earby & Bee Walker, had started one of our family traditions a few years earlier, which was to bring a gift back for each member of the family when they went on a trip. This scout trip was one of my first away from home without my parents. I wanted to be like them, so to keep the tradition alive, when my scout troop stopped at a roadside gift shop on the way to Cherokee; I went in to get my gifts. I wanted to go ahead and get them now, because I didn't want to wait until we were coming back, because I might not have enough money then to get everyone something nice.

As we got off the bus, one of my "buddies" said, "Let's see how much we can steal." Several of us went in on the deal. I wanted to be accepted – be part of the crowd and not be seen as a wimp, so I went along. Then, once the decision was made to be a thief, I suddenly saw it as a great way to get presents for each of my family members without spending any of my money, which meant I could then spend all of my money on me. How's that for "little thinking and being small - minded." - not to mention being criminal to boot.

Our foray into thiefdom was successful. We all made it back on the bus. Everybody had gotten what they wanted and nobody got caught. I stashed my ill-gained gifts in a safe place; forgot about them and went on to have a wonderful week of camping in the Great Smokey Mountains of North Carolina.

On the way back home, just a few miles away from seeing my family, I decided to dig down in my footlocker and check on my presents. As I looked through my dirty clothes and camping gear, I couldn't find my gifts anywhere. I knew I had put them deep in the bottom of my foot locker. They had been well hidden. As I came up out of that box and looked around the bus at my fellow scouts, I had to accept the fact that one of them, one of my fellow scouts. . .the same guys who had raised their right hand and pledged to be honorable. . .had stolen my gifts from me. Oh, the irony of it all! I can't begin to describe for you the feeling that came over me that day. If I think about it hard enough, I can still conjure up those emotions over forty years later. It's that desperate, hollow feeling in the pit of your stomach, when you realize you are caught doing something you shouldn't do. I rode the rest of the way home with that gnawing ache inside of me. As several of my fellow scouts grinned back at me, I began to eliminate them one by one and before we got home, I thought I knew who had stolen my stolen treasure, but I couldn't prove it.

Even worse were the feelings I had after we'd gotten home, unpacked and I had to tell my mama, my daddy, my sister and my brother that I didn't have anything for them. I'll never forget the feelings I had when they realized I didn't have anything for any of them. My dad said it was alright, but I had let him and my entire family down. I convinced myself that they felt I didn't think enough of them…love them enough to bring them even a little trinket from Cherokee.

I began to learn two lessons that day. Notice I said began to learn. I had to go through one more bit of thievery that you'll read about in a moment to fully learn my lesson. The two lessons were:

1. There is no honor among thieves

and

2. My value and belief system needed some work.

The second incident that finally cured me happened in Jr. High School. I was in the 8th grade at Wardlaw Junior High at the corner of Elmwood and Park streets, almost in downtown Columbia. One of the traditions at Wardlaw was that during recess, eighth graders were allowed to go across Park Street to a store that was on the opposite corner from the school and buy snacks. If you didn't have any money to participate in that, then you were simply a "nobody." Only those who always had enough change on them, could be considered a part of the "in crowd." I always made sure I had enough.

One morning I realized I was dead broke. Not only was I broke, but there was no hope of getting any financing either. I had already borrowed all of my next several allowances and I knew neither Mother nor Daddy would advance me even one more penny. But I knew I could not get on that bus without, at least, a few coins in my pocket.

Our home was a typical ranch style house with bedrooms and bathrooms on one end and kitchen, den, living room and dining room on the other end. When I finished breakfast, I excused myself and as I walked down the hall to my bedroom to finish getting ready for school, the devil reentered my life.

The thought occurred to me that my daddy always hung his trousers over the door (which I still do to this day) with his pockets full of everything he always had with him…a pocket knife and a handkerchief - two things he taught me a gentleman had with him at all times. Only difference is, Daddy didn't have to deal with metal detectors at airports…so I never have a pocketknife when I'm traveling. Daddy also kept his keys, his wallet and what seemed like a couple of million dollars in change in his pockets.

I knew his cache of change would be in his right front pocket and, since he had so many coins, he'd never miss a couple of them. I could hear my entire family talking in the kitchen, including Mama and Daddy. I went to the door of their bedroom and sure enough, there were his pants hanging on his closet door, all weighted down by the several pounds of change in that right front pocket. As I stood in the doorway planning my heist, I listened one more time and making sure everyone was still in the kitchen, I made a quick move to the pants, put my right hand down in Daddy's pants pocket, grabbed a couple of coins, and as I was taking my hand out, I glanced back over my shoulder to make sure no one was there and Daddy was standing in the doorway watching me. I just about lost my breath, my heart stopped, and sweat poured out of every pore in my body. The only thing I didn't do was lose complete control of all bodily functions. . . .

...but I felt like a dying man must feel right before they put the blindfold on and the last thing he sees is the firing squad.

I let the coins drop back in the pants and started easing my hand out in preparation for whatever was about to happen and also so I wouldn't come out with any evidence...who knows, maybe I could instantaneously make up a story on the spot about helping him count his money or seeing how high I could reach or that I'd gone insane and thought I was in my bedroom getting my pants down from the door but I knew any of those would only make matters worse. I'd heard him say on too many occasions that the only thing he hated worse than a thief was a liar. I didn't want to compound my problem.

I fully expected to see him reaching for one of his belts that I'd never worn, but knew all too well, because he'd about worn them out on me. However, when he heard the coins fall back into his pocket, he said, "No, son, go ahead and get whatever it was you were getting." I mumbled something like, "No, that's ok. I really didn't want anything." Lie number one. He then said, "Oh, no, put your hand back in there and get what you were going after." I tried to say no again, but he insisted and with sweaty, trembling hands I reached back in his pocket and got one coin. I guess he could tell what I was doing, so he said, "No, go ahead, since you're already there. Go ahead and get as much as you want." So, I got a couple more.

As I held them in my hand and walked over to him he looked at me with the most serious look of disappointment I had ever seen on his face and said, "I want you to go on to school and I'll be here when you get home from school. We'll talk then."

AAAAhhhh!!!! What horrors - what anguish - what embarrassment and what shame! Just beat me and get it over with - anything but the punishment of waiting, of wondering, of self-deprecation. All day long I held onto those coins. Ten guys with guns to my head couldn't have wrestled those coins from me. My daddy WOULD see his money again. Not being able to go to the store and buy a piece of candy paled in comparison to what I had waiting for me that afternoon. I beat myself up all day for what I had done. I guess that's when I learned that guilt is a great motivator.

Today, "dead man walking" is a term most are familiar with because of the movie of the same name. I didn't know the term that afternoon, but I did know the feeling. As I entered the house, daddy was waiting for me. He came over, put his arm around my shoulder and asked, "How was your day?" I remember blubbering through several I'm sorry's and that it had been a terrible day, as he led me into our living room and the family Bible with the picture of Jesus on the cover that weighed a ton, had gilded edges and always sat on the coffee table. He opened it to Exodus 20 and had me read verses one through seventeen aloud. Then he had me re-read verse fifteen – the eighth commandment. Care to guess which one that is? Then he turned the pages over to the book of Numbers and had me read Numbers 32:23 aloud. After that, he said, "I know you've probably memorized the Ten Commandments in Sunday School, but I want you to go back over them, especially number 8. I want you to make sure you know them well. I also want you to memorize the verse you just read in Numbers. When you feel you're ready, I want you to let me know, so you can share those with the rest of the family and me from memory. Then I want you to apologize to me for stealing."

As I opened my mouth to beg for forgiveness and grovel at his feet, he interrupted me and said, "No, not now – after you've made your presentation. And by the way, I want you to also apologize to the rest of the family for your selfishness and for putting us through this." Then he reached over and hugged me as he got up and left me sitting on the couch with the Bible.

I honestly don't remember what happened after that. I imagine I did ok with my memorization and my presentation and my apologies to Daddy and the rest of the family. What I do know is that since then, when at **anytime - any thought** - of **any kind** crosses my mind that includes my being involved in even the smallest bit of thievery, that incident rushes into my consciousness and stops me dead in my tracks. I became convinced that people in positions of authority could read my mind and to this very day start to fall apart, if I find myself about to steal something, whether it is money, time, other people's ideas, or anything else that is not mine.

Just think of all the good characteristics you see in others – honesty, integrity, to do your best and to provide the highest quality of service to others – and you'll see those same outstanding qualities in successful organizations. There is a company based in Columbia, SC that has developed a reputation of living by the highest values. An incredibly strong commitment to their faith, their employees, their suppliers and their customers are what have made the 6,000 employee, Southeastern Freight Lines, the great company it is today. In their over 50 years in business, they have received (as it says in their web site – www.sefl.com) over 225 quality awards from some of the most respected companies in America. They are truly a values driven company. What is really interesting is that the company is a direct reflection of their Chairman, W.T. Cassells, Jr. and their President, W.T. Cassells, lll. I'm convinced that any organization who wants their employees to operate by the highest values and standards, will only do so if the people at the top rungs of the leadership ladder are people who have clear values.

Whether I'm conducting a workshop just on values or I'm teaching it as a part of one of our other programs, there is an exercise I take the participants through that I want to encourage you to consider doing. Get out a clean sheet of paper. Divide it into three equal sections by drawing a horizontal line all the way across the page about a third of the way down from the top edge and another one about a third of the way up from the bottom of the page.

In the top left corner, write the words Retirement Banquet. In the top left corner of the middle section write Last Look, and in the top of the third section write Ten Years Later. Use you imagination and pretend you have worked for the same organization for a long time. Maybe it's the one you are with now. Retirement time has arrived and you have been a model member of your team. You've done so well that the company has decided they want to honor you at a retirement banquet. The big night arrives, the room is packed and everyone you know and work with is there, decked out in their finery. The CEO stands up and starts talking about you. In the section labeled Retirement Banquet, write down the kinds of things you would **like** to hear said about you. Others get up to speak and talk about the kind of person you were, your contributions, your attitudes, your work ethic, etc. What do you want them to say?

Then use your imagination and pretend you live another thirty or forty years and one day you are in the midst of your favorite activity. . .traveling, yachting, fishing, golfing, etc. and you drop dead. . .I'm talking, as they say: Dee Eee Dee. . .dead. There's no bringing you back. Then pretend you are stretched out in your favorite funeral home (even if you want to be cremated, will your body to a medical school, mummified, or frozen...go along with me and the traditional funeral home thing for just a moment) and there is a group of people standing over in the corner. Even if some of these have already passed away, for the purposes of this exercise, bring them back to life. The only people in this group are your spouse, parents, your siblings, and your children. They obviously, are talking about you. Write down in the second section what you would **like** for them to say about the kind of spouse, child, brother or sister and parent you have been. For some of you reading this, don't write down what they might say today, but what you would like for them to say.

Finally, it's ten years later and sitting around a table in your favorite restaurant are four people: your best friend (outside of family), one of your former neighbors, an individual you worked with, and someone who was in the same community group with you, such as a civic club, church, synagogue or mosque, chamber of commerce, etc. and guess who's name comes up - yours. In the third section, write down what you would like to think those four would say about you ten years after you are dead and gone. The first one chimes in and says, "I can't believe (your name) has been gone ten years. One of the things I really liked about ole (your name) was that (fill in what you'd **like** for each of them to say on each line)

1. (Friend) _____

2. (Neighbor) _____

3. (Co- worker) _____

4. (Community) _____

24

Once you've done all that get a clean sheet of paper and write the words "Values Statement" at the top of the page. Then begin to write your values statement in present tense language. Here are the seven areas about which you need to write something. Before you start though, you need to prioritize these seven areas as to their importance in your life – not in the order you now give them attention. I've told many an audience that if I could follow them around with a video camera for thirty days, I could tell them what their values were by the way they spent their time, what got the majority of their attention and by the way they interacted with others.

Once you've decided the order, start with the most important area of your life, then second, and so on. The seven areas are (in random order)

Health, Spiritual, Financial, Community, Professional, Family and Personal Growth

Your first sentence should begin with: I believe or I am and continue from there. Good luck as you define those values that are most important to you, that you stand for, that you are not willing to compromise, and that you would fight for. . .to the death.

The way I like to define my values is by drawing a circle in the middle of a clean sheet of paper (about the size of the bottom of a paper cup) and then draw six lines evenly divided away from the circle – like a sunburst, giving me six areas in which to write my values plus the center in which I write my spiritual values. I prefer that model because God is at the center of my life and influences everything I do. Every decision I make centers around my relationship with him. So, instead of being one of seven areas for which I've written values, it is the main area, is at the center of my life and influences all of my other decisions. I hope it is the center of your life as well.

CHAPTER 2

BIG LAUGHS

"Show me someone who can laugh at themselves and I'll show you someone who has a high level of self esteem."

One year, my friend Zig Ziglar received one of the National Speakers Associations most prestigious awards at our annual NSA convention. The Master of Influence Award is given to one person each year who we feel has had the greatest global impact with their speaking. In receiving this award at one of our luncheons, on the last day of our annual convention, Zig gave an acceptance speech that started with him thanking the five people who had the greatest influence on his life and made him who he was today. He remarked that all five were truly great women. I sat there thinking about what Zig had said and that evening when I stood up at our closing gala banquet, in front of 2,000 speakers and friends, I opened with the following:

"Since lunch today when I heard Zig thank the five women who made him the person he is today, I got to thinking about it and realized that the five people who had the greatest influence on my life were also all women. I probably wouldn't have even mentioned it, but since Zig brought it up, I feel like it is appropriate for me to express my appreciation to the five women who made me the man I am today. So, I'd like to thank Dolly Madison. . . Mrs. Fields. . .Sarah Lee . . .Little Debbie . . .and Aunt Jemima."

There was a chuckle or two after I said Dolly Madison, but by the time I said Sarah Lee everybody was laughing and the last two, Little Debbie and Aunt Jemima, almost put some of them in the floor they were laughing so hard. Now when I speak at any awards or recognition function, I weave my "man I am today" piece into my talk. Thanks Zig.

I come from a long line of very healthy, very big men. To put people at ease in our fitness crazed society, I always address the issue right up front. In fact, right after I'm introduced I promise the audience that I won't keep them long because I'm between meals now! I've been big all my life. I don't have any idea what it is to be a little fellow.

I've been on every diet known to man. The first diet I ever remember was a liver diet my mama put me on back when I was a child. Dr. Paul Watson, our family physician told her that I would lose weight, if she could just get me to eat some liver. The problem was (and still is), I hate liver. I might as well go out in the yard, get a handful of mud and stick it in my mouth and try to get it down as to eat some liver. For me, mud and liver are the same thing. My mama had the answer, though. She went to the grocery store, bought a slab of liver, brought it home, sliced it into thin strips, then sliced the thin strips into little cubes, and gently placed each cube in a metal ice tray and stuck that in the freezer. Then when those little cubes had frozen solid, she gave me a glass of water and a handful of frozen liver pellets to eat like little pills. I remember, it was just like eating gravel. That only lasted a few days, till Mama got tired of messing with it.

I've been on the grapefruit, the cantaloupe, and the banana diet; taken almost every diet pill ever made, and been through most of the highly touted programs available (I'm not naming any of them here, because I don't want to go through the aggravation of getting their permission to have their sorry ole diet in my book), including one a few years ago where all I got to eat was five packs of powder a day for thirteen weeks. That's right **THIRTEEN** weeks. Nothing else passed through my lips for thirteen weeks. I didn't even participate in The Lord's Supper (you might call it Communion), 'cause I didn't want to break the diet. In thirteen weeks I lost one hundred and two pounds. In the next thirteen weeks after the diet on nothing but water and a little bit of Breyer's ice cream, I gained back 110 pounds.

I pick up so many great stories from people and I love to share them in my talks. One I picked up from Sue Darring, CPP, at the American Payroll Association 1999 annual convention held at The Opryland Hotel in Nashville, Tennessee. She was the President and the two of us were at a head table, having lunch right before I was to speak to about 2,000 members of that wonderful association headed up by my friend Dan Maddux, their Executive Director. Sue and I got to talking about diets and she told me that she had been on the Metracal diet, but didn't like the way it tasted. The only way she could get it down was to freeze it and eat it with cookies. Is that a hoot or what? I don't know about you, but any diet that involves an oatmeal raisan cookie - I'm in!

We all know the funniest stories are taken from real life and one I love to tell is my seat belt story. As a big guy with a fairly large girth, I found it necessary to ask a flight attendant for a seat belt extender. I don't need much extra, but if I can just get 3 or 4 more inches, then I'm comfortable.

One day, I'd gotten on the plane and as I crossed the threshold of the doorway, I told a flight attendant I was sitting in 2B and would she please bring me a seat belt extender and a cup of coffee, when she had a chance. She said she'd be glad to and brought me the extender almost immediately. By the way, it has been interesting to see how different flight attendants bring me an extender. Some palm it and act like they are sneaking it to me, as if it is our little secret, which I really appreciate. While others bring it down the aisle like a dead snake, shouting at the top of their lungs, "Here you go" (fat boy implied), as all of my fellow passengers look my way."

It is kind of like when my mama used to carry me into the JC Penney Store in downtown Columbia, holding my hand and shouting at the top of her lungs, as we walked in the store, "Anybody know where the HUSKIES are? You know, the blue jeans for fat boys?" She always denies it when she hears me tell it, but that's what I remember.

Well, back to my seat belt story. One day, I was sitting in my seat, safely belted in, thanks to the dead snake the flight attendant had just brought me, reading my paper, when a couple sat down in the two seats directly across the aisle from me. She was by the window and he had the aisle seat. I really didn't notice them when they first sat down, but it didn't take them long to get my attention. What caught my ear was her loud voice. I never did get her name, but her husband's name was Roland. The reason I know that is because she must have repeated his name a dozen times in less than two minutes. She was getting on him pretty hard. She was saying things like, "Here, Roland, let me help you. Roland, I can't believe you can't get your seat belt on. Roland you need to, no, Roland, hand me the other, oh, Roland, turn this way, ok, Roland, scoot up just a little, not there Roland, suck it in."

It was about then that I glanced down from my paper and over at Roland. Sure enough, he was a big ole boy like me, and they were struggling with his seat belt. I wish you could have seen the look on his face as he tried with all his might to suck his belly in. She had one end and Roland had the other trying to get him fastened in. I was about to lean across the aisle and tell him about these seat belt extenders, but before I had a chance to say anything, he looks my way and, I guess, decided I couldn't hear, as he said to his wife, "Look at that guy. If he can get his seat belt on, I ought to be able to get mine!"

Well, all sympathy ceased for Roland. Then, I decided it was time to have a little fun with him. You need to know that since I only needed 3 or 4 inches of that extender, I had about a foot of it left over hanging down in my lap. I reached down and when my peripheral vision picked him up kind of glancing my way, I picked up that left over extender and threw it over the arm of my chair. You could have heard his head snap when he did a double take and just stared at my extra seat belt. I kept right on reading my paper as if nothing had happened and just for effect, reached down, picked up the extra footage and twirled it a time or two. Unbeknownst to me, the flight attendant had been watching all of this. She brought me my coffee and as she leaned down across me to set the cup of coffee on the divider between the seats, she whispered to me, so Roland couldn't hear, "You want to let's tell him about those seat belt extenders, or do you just want him to bust at about 30,000 feet?"

I looked over and he had apparently gotten his seat belt fastened, but you couldn't see it. It was hidden up in there somewhere and by the way he was gripping the arms of his seat and the pained expression on his face, he was in obvious pain. I looked back at her and whispered, "Just let him bust, we'll clean him up later."

In my quest for physical fitness, I have joined every health spa in my hometown of Columbia, South Carolina, at one time or another. I started going to the YMCA when I was just five years old. My dad signed me up for swimming lessons after I almost drowned in a lake at Sesquicentennial Park. I had floated out a little too far on an inner tube. When the life guard stood on his tall white chair at the edge of the lake, blew his whistle, looked straight at me, and through his megaphone yelled at me to come back closer to the shore, in my embarrassment when everyone turned and looked at me (remember Mama and the HUSKIES), instead of paddling back in, I jumped off the inner tube, not realizing I was in about 12 feet of water. The next thing I knew, I was sitting on the shore between Mama and Daddy wondering why they wouldn't let me go back in the lake with everyone else. Then one day the very next week, I find myself getting ready to take my first swimming lesson with other little boys my age who had apparently tried to drown themselves in some inauspicious way. I distinctly remember wishing I wasn't there. But when Jeep Rodgers, who has been and will always, be known as Mr. YMCA in Columbia, SC, got through with us, we could swim like fish.

Years later, Jerry Brown opened a Nautilus Gym in Columbia. I remember calling Jerry up and asking him if he could help me lose a little weight and get myself in shape. He said, "Sure, come on down. Bring your <u>wallet</u> and some loose clothing." I remember very distinctly telling him, "Jerry, if I had any loose clothing. . .I really wouldn't need you." He laughed and said, "Well, get the loosest you can find and come on down." So, I went over to Added Dimensions, a Big and Tall men's store and bought the biggest thing they had, took it to my tailor, and had him let it out a little, so I'd have plenty of room. I then packed my workout bag and headed off for my first day at the new gym. As I walked in the front door, the first person I spotted had wide shoulders, a little teeny waist, and muscles on top of muscles. You know the kind of person I'm talking about. The kind that looks like they work out four or five hours a day. . .and <u>she</u> was the cashier.

Then they took me up to the locker room and assigned me my locker. Try to picture this scene. There I am with my foot propped up on this bench and the sweat was pouring down off of me while I tried to reach down and tie my tennis shoes (a workout in itself!).

There was another guy getting ready to go work out just a few lockers down and we struck up a conversation. He was one of those people, like several I'm sure you have encountered, who, after breaking some bad habit, such as smoking or drinking or maybe they'd lost a lot of weight, are convinced that whatever method they used to accomplish this wonderful feat, is the only one that really works. At that point they become missionaries for their method. That is how he was. He told me he used to be big like me (which is exactly what I wanted to hear.). Then he went on to tell me that I needed to do two other things to get the weight off. I said, "Ok, what are they?" (As if I really believed he wanted my permission to share this revolutionary insight of his.) He then said that the first thing I had to do was to eat nothing by tuna fish, until I reached my goal weight (like I even had one). I got tickled thinking about the amount of tuna I would have to consume to get down to fighting weight. I could just see a line of 18 wheelers full of tuna coming to my house. I figure it would have looked somewhat like the closing scene in the movie Field of Dreams, when the cars were lined up for miles driving to the baseball field.

With a smile on my face, I said, "Ok, what is number two?" He then said that I needed to run, at least, five miles every day. If you've seen me you can appreciate this next comment even more, but if we've never been in the same room together, you need to know (in case you haven't figured out by now), at six feet one inch tall, I've hovered somewhere between 280 to an all time high of 450 lbs most of my adult life. So I'm a big boy, which should not cause you to be surprised when I tell you, "I'm not a runner." As a matter of fact, I've promised my family that none of us know how The Lord is going to take us off this earth, but one thing I have assured them is that they never have to worry about ever getting a phone call from someone and hearing them say, "We hate to tell you this, but we just found Mr. Walker out here by the side of the road dead with a pair of running shoes on." I know "No man knows the day nor the hour," but I have eliminated one of the ways it might happen to me.

In addition to joining most every health club in my neck of the woods, my wife and I have bought almost every piece of home exercise equipment that has ever been made. We've bought ropes and pulleys and walking sticks and special shoes and you name it, I betcha, we got it, or, at least, have had it at one time or another. I remember one of the first pieces of equipment I bought was one of those small, round, in-house trampolines. I must have gotten a cheap one, 'cause the first time I jumped on mine, it never sprang back.

Then, I got a Schwinn Air-Dyne exercise bike made by the people of bicycle fame. In case you've never seen one, it has handles that you hold on to as you are pedaling. Nothing unusual about that, except that the arms move at the same time you are pedaling. Both the handlebars and the pedals are attached to the bike's only wheel, which is suspended in what looks like a cage. Because of the way it is made, you get a wind right up in your face off that wheel. The force of the wind increases as your arms and legs increase the speed of the bike. There are two reasons for me telling you all this. Number one, if you own an exercise bike, you know, as we have learned that ours will hold several suits, a few sweaters, and a sweat shirt or two before it starts to tilt. Number two, ours has the benefit of serving as a way to exercise and keep your exercise clothes dry at the same time with the wind that blows directly on you.

The next biggie I bought was a Nordic Track Cross Country Ski Machine. I remember watching the commercial on TV. You probably remember it, too. The one that showed us a side view of an overweight guy with a beer gut on a Nordic Track and using time-lapse photography, they brought him down to nothing in about 30 seconds. I decided I could use one. So I called them up, gave them my credit card number and within a few days, it was delivered to my doorstep. If you by chance are also the proud owner of a Nordic Track, you know they are pretty much assembled when they arrive. About all you have to do is pull them out of the huge cardboard carton they are shipped in, make a few adjustments, then jump on it and glide your way to health and fitness.

I remember thinking, "This is it. This is the one that is going to do it for me. I'm gonna be like that guy on TV and before long, I'll be down to nothing, a mere shadow of myself." I got up on it. I put my left foot in the left ski and my right foot in the right ski and at the exact moment my right foot became securely implanted in the right ski, I became totally unbalanced.

You need to know, in case you do not own one of these medieval torture racks that are cleverly disguised as a piece of exercise equipment, they are slicker than glass. As I tried to regain my balance, my left ski shot out the front of the thing and my right ski went straight out the back and I started going down in a full split. In my lifetime, I've played a little football, been in a fender bender or two and had my share of bumps and bruises, but I've never known pain like I felt as I was going down in a full split. If you'd like to experience that feeling, just stop reading right now, stand up, and just throw your legs out in a full, James Brown kind of split.

When I realized I was headed to the deck, I reached for and grabbed that little rope with the cute handles you use to replicate using ski poles. That little rope is totally useless when 375 lbs. is headed to the deck. I only managed to grab one end and as I pulled on it, I jammed the other end up in the pulley wheel at the top of the machine. There is also a padded support that you are supposed to lean against as you exercise. I twisted, bent, and broke mine off on the way down as I was hollering for somebody to come help me. When the dust settled and I realized nothing was broken, I couldn't get away from that sucker fast enough. I gave it to our daughter, Amy, who lived 100 miles away in Charleston, SC, and told her we never wanted to see it again. I'm not a great athlete by any stretch of the imagination, but over the years, I've been able to hold my own at almost anything I undertook. I have bursts of brilliance on the golf course. I've have been known to play a fairly good game of tennis, am capable of tossing a ringer every now and then and play a half way decent game of HORSE on the basketball court. But nothing has ever totally whipped me, though, like that Nordic Track did. Then one day, it dawned on me why it had been able to do me in. Just in case you aren't that familiar with my home state, we didn't do a lot of cross-country skiing when I was growing up here in sub-tropical

South Carolina, so I had no point of reference and no experience of any kind on snow skis.

We do, however, have several other pieces of equipment lined up in one corner of our bedroom. It looks out over Lake Murray where we live, so you have a beautiful view of the ducks, geese, blue herons, red – tailed hawks, and whatever else is out there while you exercise. We have the Schwinn Air-Dyne™ I mentioned earlier, a weight bench with dumbbells, a treadmill, Health Glider™ and a Total Gym™.

We had a Christmas party at our home a while back and one of my dear friends, Bobby Foster, went back to the master bedroom to use the facilities, since the others were occupied. When he came back, he told me our exercise equipment looked great, but that we ought to dust it every once in a while to, at least, make people THINK we used it. I smiled, laughed, and actually thought about beating him up right there on the spot, but since it was Christmas and everything, I decided not to, mainly cause I think too much of him.

I have told many an audience at either the beginning of a convention or at the close of one, that being a part of any educational gathering, whether it's for a few hours or several days, we have hopefully been exposed to some wonderful and, hopefully, new ideas that will help us do what we do more effectively, but that those ideas were just like those pieces of exercise equipment I just mentioned. If we don't use them, what good are they? Not to mention the money and time we've thrown away.

One of the greatest realizations we can come to is to know that not only are we not perfect, but that we will never be perfect. Learn to not only accept the flaws, frailties, and shortcomings we all have but be able to see the humor in them. Who knows, it might even help us be a little more accepting of others and their imperfections.

CHAPTER 3

BIG EXPECTATIONS

"It's so easy to be cynical. It's much harder to take a philosophical point of view to be optimistic."

Yo-Yo Ma

I don't know a lot about personalities and personality disorders. I'll leave those to the psychologists and the psychiatrists. However, I do know a little about behavior. It is difficult to alter one's personality. I have had friends and family members who were able to control or, at least, mask a particular personality disorder with drugs and I've seen first hand the wonderful benefits of "better living through chemistry." Yet we all know the disorder is still present and has a fairly good chance of reoccurring, if the medication is removed. The only reason I even bring that up is to make it clear to you and every one I work with that I would never try to imply in any way, shape, or form that I understand all the intricacies of the human brain. Nor would I try to teach anyone else anything about it. I just know those that behave consistently with a positive approach to life seem to be able to Think Bigger and Live Larger than those cynics who are always criticizing, condemning, and complaining their way through life.

Behavior is another issue, though. I honestly believe that you and I have a natural behavioral style. By that I mean, when we are not under much stress and all is well with our world, we tend to behave pretty much the same way all of the time. Throw in a little stress, though, and our natural behavior will change. Intensify the stress and our behavior will change again. I didn't intend for this chapter to delve into behavior styles because we will talk more about that in chapter 10 when we discuss motivation. This chapter is dedicated to my belief that you and I make a conscious choice every morning when we get up to either approach today with an attitude of positive expectancy or one of negative expectancy. The choice is ours to make every single day.

I have living proof there are some people who go through life with a negative expectancy. If you have ever been to the Stouffer's On The Square Hotel in Cleveland, Ohio, you are familiar with the magnificent ballroom they have in this wonderful old hotel. If you have never been there, I hope you have a chance to visit it before it is torn down to make way for a cold looking concrete and steel "modern" hotel, which is what has happened to so many of the grand old hotels in America. What makes the ballroom in Stouffer's so unique is a mezzanine floor with a railing that allows you to walk out to the railing and look down onto the ballroom floor. There is also a magnificent wide staircase that sweeps down to the floor from the mezzanine.

I was attending a convention there and the first time we walked into the ballroom for our opening session, one hundred and fifty young people who were in identical outfits and ranged in age from six to eighteen years of age, were spaced out evenly around the railing with two or three on each step of the staircase. I noticed they had their own small band that consisted of a drummer, a couple of guitars, and a piano. I later learned they were "The Singing Angels" a world-renowned group from right there in Cleveland. I also learned that every year, hundreds of young people try out for the group, but only enough are selected to fill the group out to the maximum five hundred.

As soon as we were seated, the director raised his arms and when he began, those young people literally exploded into some of the most beautiful and dynamic music I have ever heard in my life. Everyone was immediately swept up in their music and throughout the room you could see people tapping their feet and moving with the music. About five or ten minutes into the concert, a gentleman sitting at my table leaned over and tapped me on the shoulder. I realized he wanted to tell me something, so I leaned back towards him, not wanting to take my eyes off The Singing Angels for fear I would miss something. He leaned up and said in my ear, "I've been listening for the past few minutes and I believe the piano is out of tune." I then

36

tried to listen to see if I could tell if he was correct. But after a few seconds, I got tickled when I realized that I don't know when a piano is in tune...much less out of tune. I quickly looked back at him with a "don't bother me again" look and went right back to enjoying the concert.

Was the piano out of tune? I don't know. Did it matter to those young people and the majority of the audience? I couldn't tell that it did. What I do know is this. I've been around this individual for a long time and he is the type that goes through life expecting bad things and guess what – not only does he find bad things, but he has become a magnet for bad things. Then, if neither of those happen, he makes up bad things, even if they aren't there. I'm convinced that gentleman crossed the threshold of that ballroom, determined to find something wrong because he seemed to feel quite proud of the fact that he had discovered a flaw.

Aren't people like him sad? Instead of going through life looking for and smelling the roses, they look for the stinkweed and the wild onions. If they can't find any, guess what the roses begin to smell like to them?

One of my favorite stories is about the sales manager who was working with one of her worst salespeople in an effort to see how she could help him be more productive. She decided to meet him early one morning and spend the day making sales calls with this individual. She met the man for breakfast and when they got in the car to go to their first sales call of the day, as they were riding along, she said, "Isn't it a beautiful morning?" Then he said, "Yeah, but you know it is raining somewhere." She knew right away what his problem was. He didn't expect to be successful. And as you can imagine, he wasn't.

There is an individual in our community who is known for her negative expectancy toward life. You can bring up any subject or share any thought or present any new idea and she'll give you umpteen different reasons why it won't work, what terrible things could happen, and then she will launch into a treatise on how sorry her family is, what a lousy husband she's stuck with, her useless children, the idiot she has for a boss, and what a sorry community we live in.

As I was starting to back out of a parking space one day she was just a few feet away from me, walking to her car. My window was down and she looked my way, made eye contact, and gave me what appeared to be a hint of a smile. That alone surprised me, because I don't recall ever having seen her smile. She always has such a sour look on her face. Then as she got almost even with my door, she said, "Hi, Al. How are you doing?"

Her question threw me into almost total shock. Here's why. I've learned that when people with her attitude toward life are engaged in conversation, it is always, <u>always</u> one sided. It is always about them and their problems. They will rarely ask you how you are doing, what is going on in your life, or anything else about you. They just want to talk about themselves. So, I had certainly never anticipated a "how ya doin'?" question to ever come from her.

Well, when she smiled and asked me that question, I was so surprised (and I'm sure it probably showed on my face) that I just had a knee jerk response. I smiled and said to her, "I'm doing great" and I should have stopped there, but I went on with my usual, "How are you?" At that moment, I would have given a hundred dollars to get the "how are you" back. I didn't realize she'd figured out a way to take negativity to a whole new level. She was now running around trapping people into listening to her diatribes and I had just become her next victim. I was driving one of those big, gas guzzling SUV's and had my window down. She grabbed hold of the side of my door and began to show me her old self. Her true colors jumped forth. She spent the next few minutes telling every ache and pain she had and let out a string of complaints about everybody and everything she could think of. I don't believe she left anybody out. She was one of those kind of people who never breathe while they are talking. It is non-stop. Not a single break in any sentence…truth is, it is just one long sentence that goes on and on, until she decides to end it. Because of that, it seemed like I sat there for an eternity, even though it was just a few minutes. The second she did stop, I just said, "yes ma'am" and mumbled something about having to be somewhere. As I drove

38

away, I realized I was slumped down a little further in my seat than usual and seemed a little depressed. Then I got tickled and started laughing as I realized I had let her have that effect on me. I sat back up and went right back to being my old positively expectant self.

We all have to decide every day, whether or not we want to have a positive or negative impact on the world. If you are a person going through life with a negative expectancy and have any desire at all to change to one with a positive expectancy, it will take some effort. I recommend you do three simple things.

First, spend a few minutes every morning before you even get out of bed and decide which person you will be that day. Second, if you decide to have an attitude of positive expectancy, quickly remind yourself of all the reasons you have to be thankful…and no matter how difficult life is, I promise you, you can find, at least, one reason to be thankful. Here's one. The God who created the universe and everything in it, the God who has been, is now, and will be forever, loves you and wants you to be happy and to have peace and joy in your life. If you are a believer, I know you know that and maybe you just need a reminder. If you are not a believer, don't dismiss it lightly. Learn more about God before you go any further. I'll be glad to help. Just email me at <u>al@alwalker.com</u> or call me at 1-800-255-1982 and I'll be happy to talk with you and send you a thought or two that might help.

Finally, throughout the day, sing a song I've heard all my life and one that was referred to a lot by one of the most dynamic ministers I've ever known, Dr. Marshall Edwards. It is a song I know you've heard before and if you don't know the tune, just repeating the words will make you feel better.

The song is "Zippity Do Dah" and the words of the chorus are:

Zippity Do Dah, Zippity Aye.
My, oh my, what a wonderful day.
Plenty of sun shine headed my way.
Zippity Do Dah, Zippity Ay.

As Marshall would always say - I hope you make every day a "Zippity Do Dah" kind of day.

You and I both know, though, that even the most positive among us gets a little down every now and then. I know this will elicit a gasp from you, when I tell you that, yes, even I have had a down time or two but the good news is they didn't last long. Thank goodness that when I have caught my self not having the positive expectancy I believe in so much, it didn't take me long to snap out of it, but if I couldn't pull my self out of it quickly, God has always sent an angel to get me straightened out. My wife has the uncanny ability to say just the right thing at the right time when she senses I need a shot in the arm. That is just one more reason why I thank the Lord for her every day.

When our daughter Amy was just two or three years old, I started taking her to our local zoo in Columbia. And by the way, if you want to visit one of the premier zoos in the world, come visit Riverbanks Zoo and Gardens. Satch Krantz, one of the nicest guys you'd ever want to meet and someone who is a good friend of mine, has been running the zoo for more than a couple of decades. He and his team of professionals have taken our zoo to a ranking of being listed as one of the top ten zoos in America. The care of the animals in their "as close to a natural environment as you can get in a zoo," the botanical gardens and the setting that straddles the Saluda River is breathtaking. (I hope my mentioning this will get me a lifetime pass to the zoo when Satch reads it.) Anyway, by the time Amy started the first grade we had made several trips to the zoo. It always seemed like as soon as we got back home, she started asking when we could go to the zoo again. We had made one of our zoo trips sometime in late August...just a couple of weeks before her very first day of school.

After she had been in school for only a few days, she started asking me when we could go to the zoo again. I said the usual; "We'll go soon, honey. We'll go soon" and that would seem to appease her for the moment. Finally, after several put offs one evening, she finally pinned me down and wanted to know EXACTLY which day were we going to the zoo. I looked at my calendar and saw I was going to be in town the next Tuesday. So, I told Amy that would be the day we would go to the zoo. We agreed that I would pick her up from school and we would head straight for the zoo and spend the rest of the day there.

A few days later, Tuesday came. This occurred sometime in late October or early November. During that time of year in South Carolina, we could have a bright, sunny, beautiful day or we could have a cool, damp, cloudy and maybe even rainy day. Well, that Tuesday, it was the latter. It hadn't really rained much, but there had been an on and off again mist throughout the morning. It was overcast all day and as I was driving to school to pick Amy up, I decided we would not go to the zoo that day, since the weather was not conducive to walking around outside. Plus, the animals would probably be back in their caves or cages or up in their trees and not out where we could see them.

When Amy jumped in the car, I said something like, "You know it's been cloudy and misty and cool all day. As a matter of fact, they probably kept y'all in from recess. So, let's not go to the zoo today. We'll go again soon though." By now, I was driving and paying attention to traffic, instead of looking at her as I talked. When I got through, she didn't say anything, so I glanced over at her. Her entire countenance had changed. Instead of being the happy little girl that had excitedly bounced into her Daddy's (or "Diddy's" as I came to be known) car, her former smile was down turned and a little tear was rolling down her cheek. That's all it took. It was over. When I saw my little girl, the child who loved me so unconditionally and whom I loved so dearly and love to this day more than any daddy has ever loved a daughter, sitting there crying, because I had changed our plans for the day, I couldn't take it. My eyes watered up, I apologized profusely and we headed for the zoo, even though I really didn't want to go walk around Riverbanks Zoo in the rain.

I learned several things after we arrived. The first was that Tuesday afternoons are a great time to visit the zoo. Nobody goes to the zoo then, so we practically had the place to ourselves. Apparently that was par for the course, because as much as Satch hates for me to tell this, we had to wake the guy up at the ticket booth so we could buy a ticket. In Satch's defense, that was over twenty years ago and the zoo is a lot busier on Tuesday afternoons now. We made the entire tour that day even though most of the animals were not to be seen, as I had predicted. Remember now, I didn't want to be there. I was only there because shortly after her birth, Amy learned that she owned me lock, stock, and barrel and has always been able to get just about anything she wanted out of me and I've given it to her gladly. But still, on this day, I would have rather been somewhere else.

As we approached the moat on the safe side of the Lion exhibit, I remember looking in and not seeing a single moving thing. Not Amy. She jumped up on the railing and said, "Diddy, look at the lions." I told her I didn't see any and she said, "Look over there behind that rock," and she pointed to a spot way at the back of the exhibit. Sure enough, almost completely hidden behind a rock was not one, but two lions. The way I knew there were two lions was because, even though you really couldn't see the lions, you could see the two lions' tails that stuck out from behind the rock. The only way you knew they were real was because one of the tails moved just a little as we watched them. However, that was all Amy needed to see to be exuberant about seeing the lions. She didn't NEED to see the rest of their bodies. Her little imagination and her memory took care of that. I'm sure in her mind, she could see those lions as clearly as she would had they been standing right in front of us.

We continued our walk around the zoo, looking at mostly empty exhibits, which didn't seem to matter to Amy. I had told Amy when we first arrived that she could have anything she wanted within reason. The minute we walked in the gate, she wanted a Coke, so I got us both one. By now, though, we had finished those and when we got around to the back side of the zoo, as we approached a food stand, she asked if she could have an ice cream cone. I got her one and got me one, too. I've always felt that it wasn't a good thing for a small child to eat ice cream all by themselves.

As soon as I handed her the cone of ice cream, she looked up at me on this cloudy, overcast, on and off misty rainy day and said to me in the way that only a little six year old child could say to her own father, "Daddy, isn't this a beautiful day?" Oh, I can't tell you how many times since then, I'd be riding in my car or be in a situation that seemed a little bleak and I'd go back to that day in the zoo, now more than a couple of decades ago and look into the face of my little girl as she reminded me that it doesn't matter if things aren't perfect. It doesn't matter if everything isn't going our way. All that matters is our attitude toward whatever situation we find ourselves. As my dear friend W. Mitchell, an incredible speaker whose body is in a wheel chair but whose spirit soars above the heads of everyone he's with, says, "In life, it isn't what happens to you that counts. The only thing that counts is what you do about it." It took a child to remind me of that lesson and I've never forgotten it. Thank you Amy and Mitchell.

As a result of that visit to the zoo and my continued effort to have an attitude of positive expectancy and have as positive an impact on Amy as I could, I had another little incident that told me she really was tuning in to all this positive thinking stuff.

When Amy was about 8 years old, I had decided the house needed painting and that I was going to do it. I don't know how many times you've painted your own house, maybe several. I had never painted an entire house before and, as a result of that experience, have not painted one since. One thing I learned is once you start painting your house, your neighbors want you to finish the job. For some strange reason, they don't like a partially painted house in the neighborhood.

I had selected the next Saturday as the day I would <u>finish</u> painting the house. I had been out later than I had intended that Friday evening, so I was a little tired the next morning and woke up regretting I had made the announcement that I was going to finish painting the house on Saturday. I got up early, though, and got all my paint, brushes, and ladder situated and started finishing this project.

You need to know that this was a fairly large house and one point was a good ways off the ground. I mention that because somebody my size had no business that high off the ground. You're talking about a guy who has a ¼ inch vertical leap here, so I've always been a little shaky, if I get too far away from good ole terra firma.

About mid morning, I'm slapping paint on as fast as I can, really aggravated that this job is taking so much longer to finish than I had planned and out the front door comes my perky little Amy with a big ole smile on her face. Immediately, in an effort to, at least, <u>look</u> like I was making the most of this stupid job, so I could make a favorable impression on my child, I put a big smile on my face and started whistling a happy tune.

Amy came and stood over near the ladder, looked up, and watched me for just a few seconds then said, "I know what you are trying to be." I said, "What do you mean you know what I'm trying to be?" She said, "You're trying to be an optometrist, aren't you?" I almost fell off the ladder laughing. Somewhere along the line she'd confused those two words <u>optimist</u> and <u>optometrist,</u> but it didn't matter. Wrong word, but perfect meaning!

Twenty years later, Amy was living in Charleston, SC, and teaching at the Ashley River School for the Arts. A couple of weeks before school started she called and told me they had been tearing the tile floors out of several of the classrooms. Hers and the other third grade teachers were included. She had just found out they were not going to finish installing the new floors before school started and the three or four third grade classes were going to have to start the year meeting together in the gym. Those teachers had decided they needed to get together and figure out how they were going to make it work.

She said that she was calling because she knew we had a lot of team building exercises that we use in our team building programs, particularly our two day, "Living and Working Together, The Art of Getting Along" program, and she wanted to know if I could go over those and any others I could think of. I immediately went to my "Games Trainers Play" books written by my good friends Ed Scannell and Bob Pike and shared several of those with her.

As we hung up the phone almost an hour later, I remember thinking, "it took." All the effort I had put into helping Amy see the value in having an attitude of positive expectancy, paid off. She could have just as easily have called me and said, "You aren't going to believe what they've done now. They've torn our floors up and have no earthly idea when they will be fixed and now we have to start the year in the gym, meeting with all the other third grade classes. Can you believe that? What in the world am I going to do? It is just not the way we have always done it and I'm certain the whole year will be messed up, because the construction people couldn't do their work on time" and on and on and on.

But she didn't. She realized there was nothing she could do to have her classroom ready by the start of the year, so she decided to see the HUGE advantage in THINKING BIG AND LIVING LARGE. Amy approached that situation with an attitude of positive expectancy, looking for what would work, instead of approaching it with an attitude of negative expectancy. It ended up being even better than she, the other teachers, or even the students and their parents had anticipated. She later told me that it was one of the best starts to a school year they have ever had.

One of the characteristics I have noticed in people who go through life not expecting things to work out is that they are always complaining about what they don't have, instead of being grateful for what they do have. Want to know what happens to people who go through life with a negative expectancy, focusing on what is not there, what might go wrong, or what they don't have, as opposed to those who are tuned in to the positives? Here is a little fable that best illustrates what can happen.

Billy and Suzie were two young people who had been dating for a couple of years. They were very much in love and Billy decided it was time to ask for Suzie's hand in marriage. He took a big chunk of his savings and bought the largest diamond engagement ring he could afford. As he and Suzie were talking one evening during the week, he suggested they go out for dinner to a very elaborate restaurant and to a concert the next Saturday. She agreed and for the next few days, Billy made his plans.

Saturday night came. Billy picked Suzie up and they went to the nicest restaurant in town. We're talking linen tablecloths and napkins, crystal stemware, 8 pieces of silver, fine bone china, and an incredible meal to boot. After dinner, they went to the concert where they had the time of their lives.

Following the concert, Billy drove to a very romantic park that overlooked the city. Billy's heart was pounding as he reached into his coat pocket for the ring. With his hand inside his pocket, holding the ring, he turned to Suzie and said, "Suzie, I love you and I want to ask you to marry me, but before you say anything, I need to remind you that neither I nor my family have much money and we certainly don't have the kind of money Jimmy Green has. My father doesn't own a business I can take over some day, like Jimmy's dad does. We don't belong to the country club like the Green's do. We don't have a spacious beach house at Pawley's Island like Jimmy's family, and we don't take annual trips to Europe, Asia, and some of the world's great resorts like Jimmy's family does. But I love you and I want to ask for your hand in marriage.

She turned to Billy and with the look of love in her eyes, she said, "I love you, too, Billy but tell me just a little bit more about Jimmy Green."

One of my favorite stories about Thinkin' Big and Livin' Large involves my two friends Dave and Bev Gorden who live in Pigeon Forge, Tennessee. Dave and Bev met in Alabama, fell in love, and were married. They tried unsuccessfully to have children for seven years. They both wanted children and had a desire to have a large family.

After seven years they decided to become foster parents. They went through the process and were approved by the State of Alabama. When they were approved, they were told it would be, at least, several weeks, if not months, before they would be given any children. Dave told me that evening they got a phone call from a social worker saying she had two little boys and that they needed to find a home for them immediately, and could she bring them over. Dave and Bev, of course, said yes.

When the door bell to their home rang, they opened the door and standing there with the social worker, were two of the filthiest little boys Beverly told me she had ever seen. They were 1½ and 2 years old. They were brothers of the same mother, but two different fathers, all of whom were either in jail or about to be. They told me they were so dirty their shoes had about taken root to their feet, since they obviously hadn't been bathed in a couple of days. Dave told me later that the oldest, the 2 year old, wouldn't even let Dave get near him for several weeks, because he had been so abused by some male in his young life.

Over the next six months I received a running account of the boys almost day-to-day activities. I was told how they were developing, how they got along with each other, how they were fitting in to their new environment, and how they both had such different personalities.

Even though I'd heard a lot about them, I hadn't met them face-to-face. When I did finally meet those two little guys six months later, they were as happy as they could be, dressed in matching sailor outfits and looking like they belonged with Dave and Bev. No one who saw them together would have ever expected anything else. As a matter of fact, one of the boys looked a lot like Dave and the other resembled Bev. The minute I saw the four of them together, it was obvious to me that the boys, Stephen and Randall, had truly fallen in love with Dave and Bev and vice versa.

I first met Stephen and Randall at the Lowes Anatole Hotel in Dallas, Texas at the National Speakers Association annual convention. If you have ever been to the Anatole in Dallas, you know that right at the entrance to the main ballroom stand two huge carved elephants that are almost life size. I'd discovered that was a great place to hang out for several reasons. It was a focal point in the hotel, so almost everybody passed by them at one time or another. It was easy to tell someone you wanted to meet to be at the elephants at a certain time. But more importantly, being a big guy myself, when I stood real close to them, they made me look a little smaller.

As Dave, Bev, and the boys approached me, I got down on one knee to meet them for the first time. I wanted to get as close to eye level with them as I could, because I've learned that a big ole boy like me can be a little overwhelming to a child, when I just bend over and speak to them. Those two confidant little guys came right up to me, we met, shook each others hands, and then I asked, "How's it going, guys?"

Before I tell you their response, let me tell you about Dave. I've known Dave for over twenty years. Every time I have ever called him on the phone or spoken to him live and in person, when I say anything that even resembles, "How you doing," "how's it going,"etc., his response EVERY time is "Terrific," If you were to call Dave right now and ask the same kind of question, I promise you he would give you the same response. At various times over the past few years, I have actually tried to throw him off in some way or get him to say something else...he won't. It's always, "Terrific." So as you can imagine, when I asked the boys, who were now 2 and 2 1/2 years old, how they were doing, they balled up their little fists, threw them up in the air, and hollered at me, "TERRIFIC!" I couldn't help but start laughing. It had taken Dave only six months to program those guys.

Six months later, Dave and Bev decided to adopt Stephen and Randall. The adoption was approved almost immediately. The social worker handling the case told Dave and Bev that the judge, who presided at the adoption hearing, had taken the two young boys back to her chambers before she made her final decision.

The judge had the boys sit in her lap, and she asked them the same question she asked every child whose fate rested in her hands. She also wanted to hear from them when there were no other adults around. She asked them, "Tell me the truth how are you really doing living with the Gordens?"

The judge told the social worker that when those 2 ½ and 3 year old boys simultaneously balled up their little fists, threw them up in the air and said "Terrific," she knew they were right where they ought to be. Today those two are confident, focused, well - mannered, young men whose destiny was impacted by one person who had made a decision years before that life is "Terrific" and was committed to sharing that conviction with the world.

Oh yeah, a few months after the adoption, Bev, one of the world's truly great Mom's, became pregnant with their third son, Samuel. All three of those young men are sharp guys who I know will accomplish some wonderful things in their lives. I've been "Uncle Al" to them now for a long time and all three of them are also champion paper airplane constructors.

Truth Seeker or Cynic.

The 60 Minutes news team once visited our National Speakers Association annual convention. That year it was held in San Antonio, Texas. We were somewhat anxious as to why they wanted to attend our meeting. They said they were there because they wanted to do a piece on motivational speakers. We were as concerned about what some of our members might do to get in front of the camera as much as we were about what they might dig up.

When word spread they were in the hotel, some of our greatest fears were realized. Several hung around unusually close to the film crews, hoping they would, at least, get a glancing shot on national television. Other antics were tried, like the one set of adult twins who were doing hand stands to get the attention of the camera crew. Luckily we were able to get some of our best for them to interview. One of them was Past President, CSP, CPAE, Cavett award winner, and former Miss North Carolina, Jeanne Swanner Robertson.

As Morley Safer was walking with Jeanne Robertson to the spot where they were to do the interview, she looked down at him (she's 6'2" and one of the most striking women I have ever known) and said, "I don't do hand stands." To reinforce his attitude toward life for you, he patronizingly responded, "I bet you would for the right price."

The show they produced depicted us in a very favorable way. One of the segments they did was an interview of Retired General Colin Powell. As they were going back stage after speaking at a positive thinking rally that had an audience of several thousand people, Morley asked General Powell, "Don't you feel guilty making the kind of money you make (General Powell's speaking fee at the time was $75,000 per talk) just to go out and motivate those people? It's just the same message over and over. . ."

General Powell responded, "You go to church every Sunday, don't you?" Implying that going to church one time isn't enough. We need to be spiritually fed on a regular basis. It was a great answer, several of us just wish he had said, "Morley, don't you feel guilty making the kind of money you make off of cynicism?" Of course, they would have cut that out and never aired it.

Doesn't that illustrate one of the great problems so many people have? Instead of having an attitude of positive expectancy, looking for the best in life, so many people have an attitude of negative expectancy and look for the worst in life. Part of going through life with BIG EXPECTATIONS means not only big expectations for yourself but for others. We call those people encouragers. I know I wouldn't be where I am today were it not for a few people along the way who encouraged me and had BIG EXPECTATIONS of me and for me.

One of them was Luther Kelley. Luther was my Dale Carnegie Course instructor way back in 1972. Luther was a tall, lanky man who always had a smile on his face. About half way through our fourteen weeks together, he told me at the break that he wanted to speak to me after class that night. I broke out in a cold sweat.

All of my academic life, if a teacher or professor ever said they needed to talk to me after class, I do not remember one single time when that turned out good. I clearly remember on several occasions when I wanted to tell them, "No, if you have something you want to say to me, or if you have something you want to do to me, say or do it now while I have witnesses."

When the classroom emptied that night I stayed behind and Luther said something to me that changed my life and made me see myself in a totally different light. He said, "Al, I've been teaching these classes for over 15 years and I've never seen anybody with the speaking talent you have. You have a gift and I hope you'll do something with it." I floated out of the room at the age of 25 feeling ten feet tall and bullet proof.

Luther and I became life long friends and he made it clear to me he had BIG EXPECTATIONS of me. I went on to become a fellow Dale Carnegie Instructor, and after I opened my own speaking and training business, Luther continued to encourage me. Every time he read an article about me in our newspaper or heard something about my speaking, he would write me a note or call me.

Often, after he retired and up until his death, I would stop by his house and visit with him and his wife Bliss. He always wanted to know where I'd been, whom I'd spoken to, and how it had gone. He'd give me another word of encouragement when I left. Ironically, I was off giving a series of speeches for an organization and was out of the country when Luther passed away. He had heard me speak a time or two and I always invited him to come hear me when I was speaking locally. I remember thinking after I got back home and had missed telling him good bye, as well as having missed his funeral, that now he could hear every speech I would ever give for the rest of his life.

To this day, I envision a second audience for every talk I give. The one in front of me and the one in heaven and I know, no matter how the audience in front of me reacts, the one in heaven is always cheering me on, grinning from ear to ear, and talking to each other about how proud they are of me...my dad, my grandparents, my speaker buddies who have passed away - Robert Henry (my life long best friend), Og Mandino, Cavett Robert, Bill Gove, Ira Hayes, Joe Charbonneau, Luther Kelley, and many others.

Another encourager and life long friend is Dutch Boling, an excellent speaker himself. Dutch was a friend of my Dad's from the days when they were both in real estate. After I had been in the training business for about four or five years, I went to Dutch just to seek some advice and wise counsel. Dutch had also been a Dale Carnegie instructor at one time. He is also the author of a wonderful book titled The Hero's Way. Call me and I'll help you get a copy.

Dutch knew I was a pretty good trainer but that something else was lacking. He pushed me to go after more speeches. He helped me see that professional speaking was the vehicle for me to utilize the gift that Luther Kelly had seen in me just a few years earlier. We even formed a group of like-minded people who were interested in professional speaking. Dutch, my sister Anne Walker, Dan McLeod, and a couple of others met on a regular basis to discuss what we were doing, how we could help each other, etc. It was what Napolean Hill would have called a Master Mind group. I also credit those folks with my being where I am today.

There is a lady who lives in Louisville, Kentucky, named Liz Curtis-Higgs. You may have heard of her. She is an outstanding speaker and author. She speaks primarily to Women's conferences. She has the label of "The Encourager." If you spent just a few minutes with her, you would agree. She really does help a lot of people see their capabilities. Lizzy is also a wonderful writer. She has written such best selling books as Bad Girls of the Bible, Really Bad Girls of the Bible, Mad Mary, Mixed Signals, half a dozen children's books, two of my favorites, Thorn in My Heart and the sequel titled Fair is the Rose. She exemplifies, in a big way, the power of positive expectancy.

Want to live a little longer? Want to spend more of your time being happy? Want more of a sense of fulfillment and pure joy? Then buy into the value of a daily attitude of positive expectancy and being an encourager…that's Big Thinking.

CHAPTER 4

BIG CURIOSITY

"If you're green, you're growing. If you're not, you're starting to rot"

I realize that rotting doesn't conjure up a pleasant picture, but it is true. Only those organisms that are green are growing and only those people who know they don't know everything and have a desire and a drive to learn are alive and growing. So, my desire is to always STAY "IGNURNT!" I realize the word ignorant is misspelled...I even had to have a word with my spell checker as I was writing this, not to mention the comments I have had to endure from my wife, Margaret, the English teacher. I've written it as **"ignurnt"** because I want you to remember it. Where I come from, that's how most folks pronounce the word. Even some of the most educated among us born and bred southerners will say about someone who hasn't quite figured things out yet, "That ole boy's kinda ignurnt." That is just the way it comes out.

The most important reason for my encouraging you to stay "ignurnt" is that the majority of people I know who seem to get along best in this world have a BIG desire to learn as much as they can. They know they don't have all the answers and are on a life long quest to acquire as much knowledge as possible. They are constantly working on their "game" whether it is in sports, business, medicine, education, or any other field. The truly successful ones know they can't ever let up. How many stories have we heard about the reporter who goes out to the practice tee at dawn to find the leader, or that year's top money winner already at work on their swing or on the putting green trying out a new putter.

My friend Jim Tunney, #32 and the dean of NFL referees, told me about a friend of his, an NBA referee, who arrived at the Boston Garden early one afternoon. He was there to call a game that night. As he headed to the referee's locker room, he heard the thump – thump – thump of a lone basketball on the court. Since it was several hours before the game, he decided to investigate to see who was on the court so early. He found Larry Bird walking up and down the court bouncing a ball over every square inch of the floor looking for any dead or weak spots that might affect his game later on that night. Here was one of the greatest basketball players of all time, an NBA All Star, a true champion in every sense of the word, out on the court all by himself. What a testimony to never feeling like you know it all.

To explain what I mean by staying ignurnt, I need to start with an explanation of the difference between ignorance and stupidity. The answer is, ignorance is curable; it's hard to work with stupid. As a loyal Gamecock and graduate of The University of South Carolina, it's appropriate at this point, since we're talking about stupid, to mention Clemson University – our in-state rival. Let me share a couple of examples for the point of illustration.

One day the football coach and the basketball coach were together in the athletic offices discussing the stupidity of their athletes. The football coach went on and on about how stupid his players were and the basketball coach argued vehemently that his were worse. They actually got into an argument over who had the stupidest athletes. Since they both believed their players were more stupid than the others, they agreed to figure out a way to settle the issue.

As they were having their debate, one of the football coach's huge linemen was walking down the hall and his coach called him over to where he and the basketball coach were standing. He gently elbowed the basketball coach and said, "Watch this." When the football player got to where his coach was, the coach reached in his pocket, pulled out a twenty-dollar bill and told the player he wanted a new car. He told his player to take the twenty down to the nearest car dealership and buy him (the coach) a car. The young man turned on his heels with the twenty in hand and left the room.

About that time the basketball coach spotted one of his tall, lanky players, and he elbowed the football coach back and said, "I'm telling you, mine are worse. Watch this." The basketball player came over to

54

his coach, looked down at him and said, "Yes sir, what can I do for you?" The coach said, "Son, I want you to go down to my office and see if I am there." The player turned and left the room.

A few seconds later the football player and the basketball player were standing out in the hall waiting on the elevator when the football player said, "I think my coach has been hit one time too many. He gave me a twenty dollar bill to go buy him a brand new automobile and didn't even tell me what color he wanted." The basketball player then said, "Well, my coach told me to go down to his office to see if he was there, and he had a phone right there beside him. He could've called."

Now that's stupid. Here's some more.

A Clemson student is walking in the sands of Myrtle Beach when he comes upon 3 coeds out sunning on the beach. "Where do y'all go to college?" he asked and they said "Yale." He then said, at the top of his lungs, "I SAID, WHERE DO Y'ALL GO TO COLLEGE?"

One day this gentleman was walking down the sidewalk and came upon a young man and said, "Son, I think I recognize you. Do you play football at Clemson?" The young man replied, "Yes, sir. I do." "How long have you been playing football?" The young man started counting his fingers and after a few seconds he said, "I've been playing for 7 years." "How old are you?" the man asked, and the young man started counting his fingers again. This time it took a little longer. Finally, the young fellow said, "I'm twenty years old." The gentleman then looked at the young man and said, "Son, what is your name?" With that the young man closed his eyes and started nodding his head up and down rather quickly, as he simultaneously, slowly moved it from side to side while nodding. After just a few seconds of that, he looked at the gentleman and said, "Kevin."

"I understand your having to use your fingers to count up how many years you've been playing football and how old you are, but when I asked you what your name was, why did you close your eyes and start bouncing your head up and down?" the man inquired. The young fellow looked back and started singing, "Happy Birthday to you, happy birthday to you, happy birthday dear…"

One of my all time favorite writers was Lewis Grizzard. He wrote a regular general interest column for the Atlanta newspaper and was hilarious. He also wrote several very funny books, such as, "Don't Bend Over in the Garden Grandma, Those Taters Got Eyes", "Elvis is Dead and I Don't Feel so Good Myself", and several others. Lewis was a graduate of The University of Georgia and a dyed in the wool Georgia Bulldog, if there ever was one. He also thought about as much of Clemson as I do and he loved to tell this joke on them.

Seems that two Clemson grads, living in South Carolina, both read the Leisure section of The State paper one Sunday and saw a $99 cruise advertised and immediately decided to go. The first one showed up at the travel agent's office early the next Monday morning. He told the guy behind the counter that he'd seen the $99 cruise advertised and wanted to sign up.

The man took his money and then came out from behind the counter, beat this guy to a bloody pulp, wrapped a blanket around him, tied him up with some rope and threw him in the river out back of his place of business. Just a few seconds later the second Clemson grad shows up wanting to sign up for the $99 cruise. The man took his money and did the same deal as before; bat, blanket, rope, and threw him in the river.

The second guy floats up on the first fellow and says, "Do they serve food on this cruise?" "Well, they didn't last year" the other replied.

Now that is really stupid.

Here's another Clemson joke. This time it involves one of their students – Bubba. Oh yeah! Just in case you are not from the South, I want you to know that the nickname "Bubba" is a term of endearment in our neck of the woods. It means – brother, friend, good – ole – boy. Why (and here's something that might get your feminist britches in a

56

knot) we even refer to some of the South's coolest females as Bubbettes.

Ok, now that we got that cleared up, let's get back to Bubba at Clemson. It seems Bubba had been at Clemson for a number of years. . .I'm talking a number somewhere in the vicinity of 12 to 15 years. Nobody really knew. They just knew Bubba had been on the campus for a long time. For the last six or eight years, Bubba had been attending every graduation, just hoping they would call his name. At the last graduation, Bubba was sitting in the stands and a chant arose from the student body, "let Bubba graduate, let Bubba graduate." This had already happened at three previous graduations and the President was prepared this time.

He called Bubba down from the stands to the cheers of everyone there and said, "Bubba, you have been going to school here a long time and just because you have been so loyal to Clemson and because you and your Mama and Daddy have become one of our biggest donors just in terms of the tuition they have paid for you over the past decade, I have decided to let you graduate, if you can answer just one question."

"I'm ready." Bubba said, "What is the question?"

The President looked Bubba square in the eye and said, "Bubba, what is two plus two?" A big grin appeared on Bubba's face as he proudly said, "Four!" At the very moment the answer came out of Bubba's mouth, the entire student body jumped to their feet and hollered at the top of their lungs, "Give him another chance! Give him another chance."

Go ahead, you fill in the blanks. That's not ignurnt, that's S _ _ _ _ D.

An edict came out one year from the FBI that they had to hire, at least, one graduating senior from every major college in America. Only one person applied from Clemson. The day after the deadline to receive applications came, the Human Resources Director at the FBI called this one "about to be a graduate" of Clemson University and said, "You were the only applicant we have from Clemson, so because of the edict, we have to hire you. However, we are required to give all applicants a test on site here at FBI headquarters. We want you to come to Washington, D.C., so we can administer the test."

When the student arrived at FBI headquarters in Washington, they immediately took him into one of the conference rooms and told him that since they wanted to make sure the Clemson slot was filled they were going to ask only one question. Furthermore, the applicant was not to answer the question until after graduation. So, the instructions were, listen to the question and do not answer until after you have graduated. Here's the question, "Who shot Abraham Lincoln?"

The Clemson senior went back to school and a classmate came up to him and said, "I heard you were going to Washington to interview for a job with the FBI. How did it go?" "Great," the student said "They already got me working on a murder case."

Here's the last Clemson joke. I have more, but I think I made my point a couple of jokes back.

Bubba was in the car with his girlfriend and he put his hand over on her knee, as they were driving on a trip from Greenville over to Clemson, down I-85. She smiled, looked over at Bubba and said, "Bubba, you can go further, if you'd like to. So he drove to Atlanta."

As a humorist, I rely on real – life experiences, rather than jokes. People prove to me every day that "truth is stranger than fiction" and is much funnier. I once spoke at The South Carolina Governors Rural Economic Conference and during my talk I brought up this subject of stupidity vs ignorance, and I used a few of the Clemson stories I just shared with you. When the talk was over, several people came up to me and had some very nice things to say. One of them was Jim Rozier, who is the County Administrator in Berkley County, which is near Charleston, SC. The county seat, and, thus, his office, is in the town of Monck's Corner, SC. Jim told me he had two real life examples of the difference between ignorance and stupidity.

The first story is about someone who was just plain "ignurnt." Jim said this elderly lady burst into his office one day, hotter than a wet setting hen. She had her purse clutched tightly up under her arm and was wagging her finger in his face. She said, "I don't know what is going on around here, but we have been faithfully paying our water bill for over 35 years, and I want to know why y'all cut my hot water off. I need my hot water and I want it back on right this very minute."

Jim said she went on and on and finally when she took a breath, he jumped in and said, "Madam, I promise you we have not cut off your hot water. We don't even send you <u>hot</u> water. As a matter of fact, we don't even send you <u>cold</u> water. We just send you water and it is up to you as to what you do with it once it gets to your house." Jim said that no matter what he said, he couldn't convince the woman the county was not sending her hot water.

When Jim realized he was about to be late for a meeting and that this water customer needed someone to get her hot water heater fixed, he said, "If you will go on back home, I'll get someone to come out to your house and take care of this." When she left, Jim called a plumber friend of his and told him the problem and that he needed to go out to the lady's house and fix her hot water heater. He also told him to explain to her how she got her hot water and to also get her to pay for his services 'cause the county wasn't going to pay for this.

Jim told me when he got back to his office later that day, the plumber called and told him that when he had called and told the plumber whom the customer was, he thought he recognized the name. Turns out that the woman's husband had recently passed away and he was the one who always handled such matters. She honestly had no clue as to how they got hot water and just assumed the county had two water lines running into her home – one hot and the other cold.

The plumber went on to tell him it was just an element in the hot water heater that had gone bad and needed replacing. Once he fixed it, he showed the hot water heater to the lady and explained how it worked. The lady then asked the plumber to please call Jim and apologize for her ignorance. She really didn't know they had a hot water heater.

Jim said the good news was that he knew he wouldn't have to worry about ever hearing from that lady again, at least, about hot water. That is a great example of "ignorance." The customer did not know about water heaters, and now she does.

Jim went on to tell me about another call he got one day from a lady out in the rural area of the county wanting him to come out and put up a deer crossing sign a little ways up the road from her house. He told her the county didn't do that and that The South Carolina Department of Natural Resources was responsible for putting those signs up because they knew the natural lanes where the deer crossed the road to get food, water, and shelter.

She said, "That's the problem! These deer out here are crossing just anywhere they please. Some cross up at one end of the road and others cross down at the other end of the road. Some cross through my yard and then others cross through my garden. I want y'all to come out here and put up one of those deer crossing signs, so the deer will know where to cross the road."

He laughed and said, "Ma'am, the dear can't read." She snapped back rather indignantly, "I <u>know</u> the deer can't read. That's why y'all put that <u>picture</u> of that jumping deer on there."

Jim said he just quietly hung up the phone. He and I agreed that is a great example of just plain ole stupid.

Here's another totally different example of stupid. One of the young men incarcerated at the South Carolina Department of Juvenile Justice related this story to my wife, Margaret, after class one day as to why he was incarcerated.

Either on TV, from one of his friends, or maybe even live and in person, he saw someone go into a convenience store, get a cup of coffee, take it to the register, and when the cashier rang it up, the perpetrator threw the scalding hot cup of coffee in the cashier's face as the cash drawer opened, grabbed a fistful of cash and ran out the door.

This "would be" criminal said to himself, "I can do that. It's easy and nobody gets hurt." He planned his crime, staked out the store he would rob, and waited until what he thought was the perfect time. As he walked in the store all excited about the big score he was about to make, he said to himself, "I don't drink coffee," so he bought a cold soda instead. and headed for the register.

How's that for stupid ?!. Can't you just see the cashier now with soda dripping down his or her face, and the look on this kid's face, when he realized he'd messed up the whole deal because of his stupidity?

Here's what I mean by "ignurnt." In 1990, we were having our National Speakers Association annual convention in Atlanta. Past President Mike Frank, CSP, CPAE and Cavett award winner was interviewing Dr. Norman Vincent Peale during one of our sessions. One of the questions he asked Dr. Peale was how had (Dr. Peale) been able to keep his energy level so high and continue to go all over the world, giving people his message of hope and encouragement for over fifty years? Dr. Peale didn't hesitate one bit. He had a BIG time response. He said there were two things that had kept him going. One was his faith in God. I expected that, since he was an ordained minister and had been pastor of the world famous Marble Collegiate Church in New York City. I was in total agreement with him on that one, because I know that the bedrock, the foundation of my life is my relationship with God. So, that response is the exact same one I would say has kept me energized and on the same path for so many years.

His second response for what had kept him energized caught me off guard, though. He said the second thing that had kept him going was that he had never lost his curiosity. I remember sitting there thinking that I probably would not have responded with that answer. Maybe something else, like, staying healthy, or helping others, or following the golden rule, would have been my response. . .but not losing your curiosity? Then it dawned on me that I was at my best and probably the happiest when I was learning something new. The challenge of going through the process of trying to understand some great truth or how to operate a computer or delving into a problem and finding some creative solution has always been an energizer for me, or as my friend Dr. Reggie McNeal would say, I get "jazzed" over that.

As a result of Dr. Peale's comment, I made a commitment to myself to never lose my curiosity. I want to keep learning as long as I live. I want to keep working on my speaking and writing and teaching skills till the day I die. I want to know the latest and greatest idea on a multitude of subjects. I like the feeling of exhilaration and excitement when I'm discovering or creating something new. I also like being around people who are on that same quest.

One of the very best speakers in the world is Jeanne Robertson of Burlington, NC, whom I've mentioned before. I know because I've followed Jeanne on platforms all over the USA, and, time after time, the people who speak to me want to know if I know her. When I tell them I do, they go on and on telling me how wonderful she is, how funny she is, and how much they enjoyed hearing her. Some even want to repeat some of her funniest stories to me. Jeanne is also a business partner of mine along with Doc Blakely, Dr. Charles Petty, Bryan Townsend and Lou Heckler in Platform Professionals. We are all southern motivational humorists. If they laugh, we're humorists. If they don't, we're motivational speakers.

I mention all of that to tell you that Jeanne has to be one of the all time greatest humorists to grace the planet. For over thirty years she has brought audience after audience to uproarious laughter. More women have had their makeup ruined by Jeanne's funny, funny stories than anyone I know, and more men have doubled over into almost sheer hysteria as they listened to Jeanne regale them with story after story about her height, her beauty pageant experiences, or her aging. Her peers consider her to be the most respected humorist on the platform today.

Why have I gone on and on about Jeanne? Here's why. No one, and I mean NO ONE, has worked harder at collecting, cataloging, and perfecting humorous stories than Jeanne Robertson. If you want to know how she does it, get a copy of her book, <u>Don't Let the Funny</u>

<u>Stuff Get Away</u>. If you'd like to get a copy, contact me (see contact information at the front of this book) or you can contact Jeanne directly at www.jeannerobertson.com. Jeanne has been a BIG time role model who has proven to me that THINKING BIG and keeping my curiosity at the highest level possible pays off...BIG time.

Here are a couple of ideas as to how you can nurture your curiosity:

Make a commitment to start reading more regularly – even just one book a month will get you through 12 books in a year. Obviously, you can double that with 2 books a month.

Maybe there is a particular course at one of your local schools you've been thinking about taking, put this book down and call them right now. Better yet, why not start working on that degree you've been threatening to finish for several years now.

Ok, that's two ideas. I know you can think of other ways to satisfy your curiosity. Good luck on your quest.

Chapter 5

Dream BIG Dreams

"Go ahead, shoot for the moon because even if all you do is clear the treetops, at least you would have proven to the world you can fly."

Speaking of flying, one of my favorite stories about dreaming BIG comes from my buddy, Bobby Foster. Bobby, like me, is a native South Carolinian. However, Bobby, UN-like me, was, and is, an excellent golfer. He was a SC Amateur Champion and later a golf coach at The University of South Carolina, and today spearheads a golf ministry to young people in addition to being a successful business consultant, trainer and speaker.

Bobby was in college during the Viet Nam era and when circumstances indicated there was a pretty good chance he would be drafted into the US Army, Bobby got a jump on them and joined the Air Force, where he was trained as a jet fuel specialist. When his training was over, he got real lucky and ended up being stationed at Shaw Air Force Base in Sumter, South Carolina, just 45 miles from Columbia.

Shortly after he was there, he was climbing up the side of a jet fuel tank when a Tec sergeant below hollered up at him and told him to freeze right where he was. He then told Bobby to slowly work his way back down the ladder and take off the fleece jacket he was wearing, because the slightest bit of static electricity in that fleece could ignite that tank of jet fuel, and they would find pieces and parts of Bobby in the mountains of North Carolina and in the marsh down around Hilton Head.

Bobby told me he was shaking when he got back down on the ground, realizing how close he had come to a terrible disaster. He decided to start looking for another job in the Air Force. He went on to say that he had seen a notice on a bulletin board that they were looking for someone to run the golf course at Shaw. Bobby had always had BIG dreams of being the head guy at a golf course and this seemed to be his chance. Plus, he knew that if he could get this job, it would take him out of the jet fuel business, at least, for a little while.

He went to the golf course, applied for the position and was notified that the base commander wanted to play a round of golf with Bobby to see what kind of golfer he was. Bobby told me he played the most inspired round of golf that he had ever played in his life. His BIG dream came true. Bobby spent the entire four years of his Air Force career managing and, as he said, keeping the Viet Cong off the golf course at Shaw. Isn't it amazing the different events in life that sometimes motivate us to do what we would rather be doing to begin with.

One of my all time favorite movies was Karate Kid starring Ralph Macchio as Daniel and Pat Morita as Miyagi. There is a scene in that movie that, the minute I saw it, I knew it would be a terrific example of what it means to clearly see what you want in your mind, then have the confidence to go after it.

In the opening scenes, the character Daniel has just moved to California from New York city with his mom. They are living in an apartment and one evening he rides his bike to a beach party. He doesn't exactly fit in and on the way home on his bike, he realizes he is being pursued by a group of guys on motorcycles who were at the beach party. They quickly catch up with Daniel and run him off the road down a steep embankment. He tumbles head over heels and his bike is bent up and damaged to such an extent that he can't ride it home.

The next scene opens with him throwing his bike in the dumpster at his apartment complex. He is angry and obviously upset over what has just happened. What he doesn't see is Miyagi, the maintenance man at this complex, standing behind the screen door to his work room and watching everything Daniel is doing. About that time, Daniel's mom pulls up in her station wagon, sees Daniel and his black eye and bruises, and jumps out to help her son. Miyagi watches as she puts her arms around him and they head up the stairs to their apartment.

The next scene opens with Daniel going off to school and the things that happen to him that day, as a result of the previous evening. Later that day, when Daniel gets home to his apartment, as he goes up the stairs to the second floor, there on the landing at the top of the stairs, he sees his bike…all fixed up, repaired, repainted, and looking like a million dollars. He couldn't believe it and remembered having seen Miyagi around the place and figured out that he was the one who had fixed his bike.

Daniel is then seen knocking on the screen door to Miyagi's work room and Miyagi tells him to come in. He thanks Miyagi who responds with a quiet, "you're welcome" and then Daniel proceeds to talk to Miyagi about what had happened to him. He describes how the guys on motorcycles came after him and how he wished he knew how to defend himself and fight better. Miyagi then offered to teach him Karate and Daniel shrugged and said, "I can't do that."

With that response, Miyagi told Daniel that he could do anything he made up his mind to do and to prove it, he told Daniel to sit at his work bench on a stool that was there. Miyagi had been trimming his banzai trees and still had several to do. He put one of them in front of Daniel and told him to trim it up. Daniel's response was the same as it had been earlier. He said that he didn't know how and couldn't do it.

Miyagi said rather firmly, "Daniel, close your eyes," and Daniel did. Miyagi then said, "Daniel, I want you to picture one of those little banzai trees exactly the way you think it ought to look after it is trimmed. Picture every leaf, every limb, the trunk and even the dirt and little rocks in the pot. Can you see it?" he asked. "Can you see it clearly?" he asked again. You could tell Daniel was concentrating and in just a few seconds a smile began to form on his face and you could see his entire face begin to light up, as if he was seeing something of infinite beauty and was thoroughly enjoying it. At that moment Daniel said, "Yes, I can see it."

Miyagi waited just a second or two more, then whispered, "Daniel, do your picture." Without saying a word Daniel opened his eyes, picked up the small pair of trimming shears Miyagi had given him earlier and slowly moved them toward the untrimmed banzai tree. But before he could make his first snip, he put his trimmer down, looked over at Miyagi and asked, "But how do I know if my picture is right?" Miyagi saw the wonderful teaching opportunity before him and with a small smile of confidence and a far away look in his eye said, "Daniel, if the picture for that tree comes from inside your head and it is your picture, I promise you, it is always right."

I wanted to jump out of my seat in the theatre and shout to all of those around me, "Did you get it? Did you get it?" Miyagi is saying that whatever we can clearly see in our mind's eye, we can make happen. But more importantly, our BIG dream for our life is always right for us, only if it is our dream; only if it is our picture of what we want to become and not someone else's, and if we can see our BIG dream clearly. I really want to encourage you that if you don't have a BIG dream for your life, get one, and when you do, it needs to be HUGE and THE BIGGER THE BETTER

My youngest brother Wes Walker played Little League baseball right across the street from our house. There are fourteen years between Wes and me, so when he was playing Little League, I was in my early twenty's. The coach of that team was a man I knew as Mr.Blocker. He had a son, Terry who played on that team and he is the young man I want to tell you about. I remember being at one of Wes' games and after it was over, I was talking to Wes, Terry, and a couple of other players, and I asked them what they wanted to be when they grew up. If I remember correctly, several of them said they wanted to be Major League Baseball players. If it wasn't all of them, it was, at least, most of them. I do distinctly remember Terry telling me he wanted to be a professional baseball player and when he said it, his voice had a little different sound of conviction to it than those of the other young people that day.

I knew Terry and his Dad were baseball fanatics. When baseball season was over for the summer and the other guys started thinking about the approaching football season and started tossing the ole pigskin around, Terry and his Dad, just the two of them, would be out on the baseball field across from the house. Terry would be in the outfield shagging fly balls Mr. Blocker hit to him, or he'd be in the infield, taking as many grounders and line drives and pop-ups as his Daddy could hit before he wore them both out. Then Mr. Blocker would pitch to Terry and he'd hit one baseball after another till his hands hurt, then they would go home. Then they'd be back at it the next day, day after day after day.

Twenty years later I was in a hotel room somewhere in the USA and I had the TV on as I did most of the time when I was in the room. This was back during the mid nineteen eighty's and thanks to Ted Turner; you could watch an Atlanta Braves baseball game anywhere in the country. Only problem was, back then the "Bravos", as some called them, weren't doing very well. It was late in the season and they were announcing the starting line up. I was kinda half listening and half not listening while I was doing something else, but I distinctly remember hearing the announcer say, "Starting in center field today for the Atlanta Braves is Terry Blocker." I couldn't believe my ears. I jumped up and sure enough, there was Terry Blocker from Columbia, SC. The same Terry Blocker who had played Little League Baseball with my brother and the same Terry Blocker who had told me very confidently, that some day he would be a professional baseball player.

A chill ran down my spine because I knew I was witnessing a dream come true. Terry had been playing in the minors and they had called him up to the BIG SHOW as they call it. BIG dreams *will* get you in your BIG SHOW. I know first hand.

In 1977, I had been in the training business only a couple of years. I was 30 years old and moving along professionally at a pretty good clip. It was in the fall of the year and we were having our annual planning meeting where we agreed on our one year sales and training plan and our three and five year projections. When we finished, the man I was working for, Walt Farrer, asked us to get out a clean piece of paper and to write down on that paper where we wanted to be professionally in twenty years. Whatever year it is when you are reading this, think ahead twenty years. What year is it? Two

Thousand and what? Well, I thought ahead twenty years to 1997. I would be fifty years old and would have been in the training/speaking business for over twenty years. Walt also asked us to write down, at least, three objective qualifiers that anyone could look at in twenty years to determine if you had achieved your BIG DREAM for your life.

Truth is, I had already been thinking about what I wanted to be doing. I wrote it down and I wrote down three objective qualifiers, just as he had asked. I thought that when we finished this little exercise we would simply fold those pieces of paper up, stick them in our pockets and head on home. Oh, nooooooo! Walt wanted us to share them with the group. My heart skipped a couple of beats for two reasons. Number one, the six of us sitting around that table were good friends. We worked together almost every day. We were a pack of young, aggressive, "take no prisoners" kind of guys (and yes, it was an all male group back then) and we loved to take cheap, sarcastic, and sometimes even caustic, verbal shots at each other whenever the opportunity presented itself. Because of that, I knew John Evans, Bob Johnson or one of the other guys, would rip my twenty-year dream to shreds and give me several dozen reasons why it wouldn't happen.

If you could have overheard us taking all the verbal jabs at each other that we were known for, you would have thought we hated each other. But the opposite was true. We were very supportive of each other and I knew I could count on any one of them at a moment's notice and they knew they could count on me. We were a great team.

The second reason my heart skipped a beat was because my BIG DREAM didn't include my boss, Walt Farrer. That made me feel a little uncomfortable. Plus, it caused me to be a little concerned about my next paycheck. Not to mention disappointing someone I truly admired.

However, when it came my turn, I told them that in twenty years I wanted to be traveling all over the country, talking to all types of people, and giving them ideas they could use to be more productive, and to give them a message of hope and encouragement. I went on to share my three qualifiers, which were - that by December 31, 1997 I would have spoken in all 50 states. I'm not talking about catching a plane to New Hampshire, going into the terminal and saying hello to a few folks and getting back on the next flight out, I mean speaking professionally to a group of people for a fee. I don't remember the second and third qualifiers exactly, but I do remember I had written down that I wanted to be averaging a certain number of talks per year. The third qualifier was that I would be averaging a certain annual income.

December 31, 1997, has long since come and gone. It marked the date, by which, I planned to achieve my first twenty year BIG DREAM. Did I make it, you ask? No, I didn't. In those twenty years I had spoken professionally in 46 of the 50 states in America. However, I had also spoken to the owners of the Eight til' Late convenience stores out of Great Britain and several times in Canada, Mexico, Puerto Rico, The Bahamas, and on cruise ships, none of which I had included in my twenty year dream. I am convinced that I would not have spoken in forty-six of the fifty states had I not been shooting for fifty. Plus, I obviously didn't dream big enough, since I hadn't included any of the "out of the USA" programs I had during that time. On top of all that, I had no idea back in 1977 that the 4000 member National Speakers Association even existed, much less that I would join in 1982, be elected to the Board of Directors in 1986, serve as President for the year 1992-1993, and receive almost every designation and award the organization gives, including the cherished Cavett award given to only one member each year for displaying the spirit of "caring and sharing", as our founder Cavett Robert called it.

I've witnessed that so many times in others. I remember sitting at a head table with the president of a large lumber processing company, as we looked out over his 250 to 300 managers that were scattered all up and down the east coast from Maine to Florida. He was in his early sixties and his father had started the company. When he took it over, it was a small company operating only in North Carolina. I asked him if when he started leading the company, if he had any idea that someday he (the company) would be as big as he was. He paused for just a moment and then looked at me with a distant look in his eye and said these exact words that I have never forgotten. He said, "No, because I didn't DREAM BIG enough."

I told him part of what I planned to talk about that evening had to do with Dreaming BIG DREAMS and would he mind if I shared what he just told me. He told me he wouldn't mind, so I added it to my speech right there on the spot. What an impact it had. He stood with me after the evening was over and manager after manager came up to us, told me how much they enjoyed my talk, which I appreciated, but, more importantly, they turned to him and made some comment that had to do with promising him they would dream bigger dreams for the company. WOW!!! There's serendipity for you.

Early one Sunday morning I had the TV on and as I flipped through the channels, I stumbled across the Hour of Power, and Dr. Robert Schuller was interviewing a Rabbi. He was asking the Rabbi what the meaning of life was and the Rabbi said, "ahog" and Dr. Shuller said, "Ahog? That is a Hebrew word I do not know. What does it mean?" The Rabbi laughed and said, "It's not Hebrew. I mean a big, fat, hairy ole hog of a dream. It must be something so big and obtrusive that you can't get away from it and you spend all your days pursuing it. Then when you get wherever that is, you create another "hog." When I heard it I said, "Right on!" That is another wonderful way of saying what I have been preaching for so long. Get a BIG OLE WHOPPER of a DREAM and hang on till you get there. Then, when you arrive at the achievement of that dream, go after another BIG DREAM.

Being a BIG DREAMER has led me to others who are cut from the same cloth and one of those is a man named Chris Weaver. I first met Chris in Las Vegas, Nevada when I spoke to a group of his top sales producers. Chris was in charge of all sales for Capital American Insurance, based in Cleveland, Ohio. We hit it off immediately. Chris is one of the brightest people I've ever known. He is always thinking. He is a high energy person, full of enthusiasm for what he does and easily gets others caught up in the pursuit of excellence.

Shortly after Chris and I had met, he told me he wanted to create a sales training program for his 8,000 sales agents in the field. We immediately went to work and began putting people through the program at about 25 to 30 agents at a time. We tracked the sales of the people who had gone through the program and those who had not. The difference was amazing. The one's who had learned how to sell professionally, increased their sales significantly over their previous levels and far exceeded the sales of the agent's who had not been through the training. Conseco bought Capital American and moved Chris and a number of the people from Cleveland to Indianapolis, Indiana. All the while, Chris is thinking and DREAMING.

Chris and I did not talk for several months and that turned into a couple of years, then one day I got a phone call from Linda Teets, Chris' right hand and one of the most professional people I've ever known, telling me that they were now in Dallas, Texas. Chris had bought out the largest agency in the Capital family and renamed it Performance Matters Associates or PMA and he wanted me to come speak to his people. Chris has since grown that agency to be even bigger and now serves customers in 45 states. Go to their web site at www.pmanews.com and you'll see this quote about their values.

"We're a team of go-getters who set goals and go out and make them happen. Achievement. Success. Dreams. That's what people find through PMA."

Chris and his team of outstanding pros are a wonderful example of what can happen when you DREAM BIG.

There is an excellent book I want to recommend to you, and do not let the title discourage you from getting the book. The title is Golf Is Not a Game of Perfect by Bob Rotello, who was director of Sports Psychology at The University of Virginia for 20 years. The book is not about golf. It is about life. The second chapter is about dreaming. He tells the story of working with Pat Bradley, one of the LPGA's best known golfers. He was talking to her back in the early nineteen eighties and he asked her what her BIG DREAM was. She said she wanted to be admitted to the LPGA Hall of Fame. He told her that was a wonderful dream. To make it come true, she had to win thirty tournaments and two of those had to be from the major tournaments, such as the US Open. Now they use a point system, but back then it was thirty tournaments and two had to be majors.

Pat Bradley was admitted to the LPGA Hall of Fame in 1992. However, both Pat Bradley and Bob Rotello discuss in that chapter of his book how between 1992 and 1994, when the book was published, Pat had not won another tournament. They agreed the reason was that she had a HUGE DREAM, accomplished it, and then didn't follow it with another BIG DREAM. They went on to talk about the importance of always having a huge dream for your life out in front of you.

One of my favorite BIG DREAM stories is about Felton Burton. I first met Felton in the early 1980's when I was conducting a series of workshops for all supervisory/management personnel at the South Carolina Department of Transportation. At that time, SCDOT had eight regional offices scattered throughout the state. Each class was made up of these key people from the various departments within SCDOT, including Highway Patrol, Engineering, Highway Maintenance, etc.

One of the regional offices was located in Greenwood, SC, and that is where I first met Felton. He had been with SCDOT for over 30 years. The program I was teaching was a full day workshop on leadership with a focus on behavioral styles. As soon as I stopped for lunch, Felton came rushing up to me and asked me if I had any plans for lunch. I told him I didn't, other than the certainty that I would eat something, somewhere. He invited me to go to lunch with him and I accepted.

The SCDOT office was on the outskirts of Greenwood and when we got in Felton's car he headed downtown. He immediately started telling me about the place we were going to eat. He had a big grin on his face as he told me the following story.

Felton and his wife Doris had five children. The fifth child was a girl they named Debbie. Debbie was the sweetest, most loving child you would ever want to be around. Debbie had Downs Syndrome.

When it was time for Debbie to start school, Felton and Doris didn't want to send her away to school, so they got a few other parents in their area together who had children with special needs and decided to hire their own teacher. It wasn't long before more parents with special needs children heard about Felton's efforts and more teachers were hired. Financial support came from various sources including the State of South Carolina. The Piedmont Multi-County Mental Retardation Center was now a full fledged effort to provide education and training for special needs children. Felton was the part - time director, while still working at the Highway department.

By the time I met Felton, the organization had purchased and totally refurbished an old elementary school in downtown Greenwood, SC, had changed their name to The Emerald Center, and had at least 100 clients that ranged in age from pre – kindergarten to older youth. Their needs varied from those who were totally incapacitated to some you really wouldn't know were any different from other children until you worked with them.

As we went into the cafeteria, children of all ages came running up to Felton, hugging him, and he was "lovin' on them" and hugging them right back. Then Debbie came in the cafeteria and went straight to her Dad. Felton introduced her to me and that's when I began a friendship with Felton, Debbie, and The Emerald Center.

Following lunch, Felton took me on a tour of the school and it was wonderful. You could feel a lot of love and energy throughout the facility. Everywhere I went, their clients (as they refer to them) came up to me with warm smiles and a hug. Felton lit up like a Christmas tree as he told me how years ago when he hired the first teacher for Debbie, he had dreamed a BIG DREAM of having a school someday that would serve the needs of every special needs child in and around the Greenwood area. And here we were walking around in the middle of Felton's dream. The more he talked the more energized he became. His level of excitement could also be seen in every staff person I met. Felton and everyone around him was on fire for these young people.

As we headed back to the SCDOT office and the afternoon session of the workshop, The Emerald Center was all we talked about. Not one word was said about the highway department. I asked Felton what his plans were. He said that one day he wanted to retire from SCDOT and work full time at The Emerald Center. I asked him how long he had been with the highway department, and when he told me 30 plus years, I asked him what seemed to be a very logical question – Why don't you go ahead and retire now?

It was obvious to me where his heart was. He wanted to be back over at The Emerald Center, living his BIG DREAM. He went in the next day and turned in his retirement papers. To this day, he tells people that Al Walker made him quit his job at the SCDOT. Felton was teetering so close to the edge that all I had to do was just barely nudge him and HE made the right decision for himself, and he has never regretted it. He realized his body was working one place and his heart was somewhere else. All he did was put his body where his heart was.

I went on to conduct some in-service sessions for the staff and got to know Debbie. Debbie was a talented painter. I told her that I had been collecting clowns for years and asked if she would paint me a picture of a clown. One day a few months later, Felton told me she had completed the painting, but I couldn't have it, because he couldn't bear to part with it.

Debbie passed away a couple of years ago and I've thought about her many times since then. I read about and hear people talking about leaving a legacy. I don't know if Debbie ever realized that The Emerald Center exits today, serving, and having served hundreds of people, helping them have a better quality of life, because she came into our world and caused one man to dream a real whopper of a BIG ole DREAM.

My wife Margaret and I were again watching television one Sunday morning as we prepared to go to church and the guest speaker on the Hour of Power program was Dr. Bruce Wilkinson, author of several books including The Prayer of Jabez. He was talking about the importance of Dreams and he made several great points.

One was that when God gives you a dream, it is always too big for you to do; but, so what, because if you truly believe your dream for your life is what God dreams for your life, then everything is already in place for you to accomplish that dream right now. You don't have to know what those are or even how to accomplish your dream – just commit.

He used Psalm 139 and I want to encourage you to read it; especially verses 13 - 16. In this beautifully written chapter, David talks about how he knew beyond any shadow of a doubt that God had made him, was watching over him and already knew everything that would happen in his life.

There is the answer to seeking and fulfilling your Big Dream for your life. If you surrender your life to God and seek His will, do you think for one moment he would have you doing something you hate?

Dr. Wilkinson's other point was that when you do know that you have latched onto your really Big Dream for your life the dream will always be outside your comfort zone. He went on to say that the wall of fear is at the edge of your comfort zone. Then he said, "Don't focus on the fear, focus on the dream."

Dr. Wilkinson concluded with, "Stop being afraid of being afraid. It is the will of God that we follow our dream."

Another of my Big Dreaming buddies is Michael Hannon who is married to the lovely, talented and beautiful Debbie Hannon. Michael has been pushing himself all of his life. He is one of the most successful sales executives I've ever known. He is now the President of The Hannon Company and provides top drawer training for sales people and sales executives. In addition to his legendary sales and management abilities, the part of Michael that I admire most is his ability to dream BIG dreams and see things others don't see.

The first time I met Michael, he was in charge of sales at Sawgrass outside of Jacksonville, Florida. It was during my time there that I learned about Michael fulfilling a dream of creating a foundation that turned an average elementary school into an outstanding elementary school. Through his BIG dreaming efforts, thousands of dollars were raised to improve the grounds and the interior of the school, but more importantly to bring big name musicians, dancers and other artists to the students that they would have never seen otherwise. How much impact did Michael's BIG dream have? He got an entire community involved in education. He raised the level of pride the teachers and the students had in their school by several degrees and he still has me talking about it fifteen years later. Today you can check Michael out at www.hannonco.com

As you can see, these past few pages have not been about annual, quarterly, monthly, or even daily goals, even though I'll be the first to tell you they are critical to our success. This chapter is about having a BIG DREAM all the time. Having a BIG DREAM keeps us focused and makes it easier to establish our goals "in" life.

As I approached 1997, and the end of my twenty year DREAM, I knew I had to have another dream right behind it and I did and am pursuing it at this moment. You are holding part of my BIG DREAM in your hands right now.

I want to be able to walk into a bookstore and be able to see my books sitting along side the books of other speakers and authors. Not because of some ego trip I've decided to take, but because I believe, with all my heart that God wants me to share what little wisdom I've picked up over the years with as many people as I possibly can and share a few laughs along the way. I even know how many books I plan to write and their titles. Who knows where that might lead. I don't have a clue but the good news is, I do know who is leading me.

Will I get there? I have no idea. All I know is that, in addition to my faith in God, having a BIG DREAM has pushed me to be where I am today. I promise it will do the same thing for you. As a matter of fact, I would love to hear from you about your BIG DREAM, whether it is one you have had for some time or one you come up with as a result of reading this. My email address is al@alwalker.com or my fax number is 803 345-1049.

CHAPTER 6

BIG PERSISTENCE

"It's not whether you get knocked down, it's whether you get up that counts."
Vince Lombardi

In 1974 I went through a separation and a subsequent divorce. I was a young man of 27. With my father's death from cancer that year, the business we were in together began falling apart at the seams. Plus, I did not like the business; my heart just wasn't in it. My mother, Bee Walker, who had worked side by side with my dad for a number of years, decided that she didn't want to continue the business the way it was either. With all of that going on around me, I knew my life was in for some major changes.

Since everything I had known was now changing, I decided that I should consider a change of scenery. I went to visit a friend of mine that I had gotten to know through taking (and subsequently teaching) The Dale Carnegie Course. As I visited him in his home, I confided my feelings to relocate. I felt the best thing for me to do would be to pack as many of my possessions as I could in my car, fill up the gas tank, and drive as far west as I could. Then when I ran out of gas, wherever that was, I would fill up one more time. When I ran out the second time, wherever I was, that's where I would begin life anew.

My friend's name is Bob Johnson who now lives in Australia (talk about relocation!), with his wife Shane. When I finished telling Bob my tale of woe, he told me a story, which, incidentally, inspired another book I co-authored with Joe Batten, CPAE. The story is about two young men who were caught stealing sheep in a village long ago. The villagers decided the appropriate punishment for the two young men would be to brand them on the forehead with the letters ST for Sheep Thief. So, it was done.

One of the young men in embarrassment, shame, and frustration with himself and everything around him, decided to pack his

78

belongings and leave their village. He traveled from village to village; yet, invariably, someone would always find out what the brand on his forehead meant, and he would leave again. He died several decades later. . .

About the same time a visitor was walking down the side walk in the village where the two young men had originally lived. As he passed one of the townspeople on the sidewalk, he noticed the faint hint of a scar on the man's forehead. He stopped a shopkeeper who was out in front of his business sweeping the sidewalk.

He asked the shopkeeper what the brand ST on the forehead of the older gentleman that he had just passed stood for. The shop keeper had been there all of his life and he knew what the ST stood for. However, as he reflected on the exemplary life the branded man had lived, how he had worked tirelessly in the community and built several successful businesses, he said, "The ST on his forehead? It stands for Saint."

Bob's insightful retelling of this wise, old tale was inspirational. That story helped me realize that I needed to stay right where I was and make my mark in life in my home town. Once back on my feet and successful at whatever I was doing, I could move somewhere else. But to run away now was not the answer.

Here's the rest of the story. About 12 years later I was traveling all over the country and seriously considered moving to Dallas, Texas, so that it would be easier and less time consuming to fly out of a major airline hub like the Dallas/Fort Worth Airport. Plus, living in the Midwest would give me better accessibility to the major markets on the west coast. The big difference between then and twelve years earlier was that this time I would be going to something, as opposed to running from something. I have shared that story with so many people, young and old alike, who felt that life just hadn't turned out the way they wanted and they impulsively felt the need to run away. Why do people think that if they can't make it where they are, they can make it somewhere else. Oh, I know, some opportunities are available in other places that might not be available where you are. For instance, if you want to be an actor, New York or Los Angeles might be a better place to live, even though we all know of actors who built a reputation in other places and then went to the theatrical hot spots with a winning track record.

Two of my all time favorite movies are Braveheart and Gladiator. They both gloriously illustrate what one very focused and determined individual can do for his country in the pursuit of freedom and justice. It is a classic example of the impact one person on a mission can accomplish. They both showed the power of being persistent in the face of incredible odds and how that persistence paid off in the end.

Another movie in a totally different genre is titled Rudy. If you've not seen it, please do. It is the true life story of Rudy Ruettiger, a young man who always wanted to play football at Notre Dame. Even if you are not a sports fan, you will enjoy this movie. The only problem with Rudy was that he was just not big enough to play football at that level; he wasn't that fast and his claim to fame was that he would try to tackle a locomotive, head on if his coach wanted him to. He never missed practice, always gave everything he had and never played in a game until the last few minutes of the last game his senior year. He would not quit, would not give up, or give in to others who told him he'd never make it. His reward, besides the self satisfaction of sticking with his heart's desire was that his teammates carried him off the field on their shoulders – something that has not been done since. He proved that you don't have to be a superstar to achieve success; you just have to stick with it. . .whatever "it" is for you.

So, whatever you do, don't quit. One of the secrets of some of the world's most successful people is that they didn't quit when the going got tough. That was when they took a deep breath, sucked it up, and charged ahead. There is a poem that I think best illustrates the value of pushing on. It is titled "Persistence." If after reading it you would like a copy, just go to my web site, www.alwalker.com and print it out.

PERSISTENCE

Two cute little frogs from inland bogs, had
spent the night just thinking.

When morning broke, they both awoke with
eyes bloodshot and blinking.

For time was had to gather senses
or breath a prayer for past offenses,

A farmer frail came down to the swale and
caught them quick as winking.

Now the farmer was a guileless man
and threw both the frogs in a huge milk can.

Well, the can filled up and the lid came down
and both the frogs and the milk were shipped
to town.

Our friends began to quiver and shake and
sober up on a cold milkshake,

For now they had to kick and swim
until their bleary little eyes grew dim.

At last one of the frogs cried out in dread, he
said, "We're gonna drown in here. We're as
good as dead."

"For shame, for shame," the other one replied,
"A frog's not dead until he's died.

"I'm gonna keep on kicking, that's my plan
and we may yet see outside this can."

"No use, no use," faint heart replied
and with a groan he quickly died.

But the other frog, undaunted still,
kept on kicking with a firmer will

and finally with joy too great to utter,
found he'd churned himself a lump of butter.

And hoping up on top of the grease,
He floated around with the greatest of ease

Now the moral of the story is:

When things are tough all over town, don't
give up and don't go down,

just keep on kicking, don't cry or mutter, cause
one more kick

might bring your butter.

I (and others) have searched high and low for the author of this poem. Let me tell you what we found out. The poem is based on a centuries old Russian folk tale about two frogs that were hungry and found themselves on the back porch of a farmhouse. The farmer's wife had put a pan of milk on the porch for the family cat who was nowhere to be seen. The frogs crawled over into the pan of milk and realized the sides were too slippery for them to get out. One of them gave up and drowned, while the other one just kept on kicking in an attempt to get out. All the kicking churned up a lump of butter. The frog jumped up on the butter and hopped out of the pan of milk. It had the same moral...don't quit. Years later, some creative soul somewhere devised the poem from that story.

I'm glad he did, because I have been sharing that poem with audiences for over twenty years, and it is on my website. We also had a cartoon booklet and a coloring book made for it. The poem with its words of encouragement for diligence and the devotion to the pursuit of a worthy ideal, has made a difference to me and apparently to others. Here's a story of how it made a difference in one family.

I was sitting at my desk one day opening the mail and as I opened an envelope from someone in Virginia, a copy of the frog booklet fell out. It was dog eared, had ink scribblings in several places, a few coffee stains and it generally looked as if it had been run over by a truck. As I opened the three page letter accompanying it, my eyes began to water.

The letter started with, "Dear Al, you'll never know the profound impact you have had on our lives." I stopped reading. No one had every told me that before. A lot of wonderful people have written some extremely nice evaluations following one of my keynote or luncheon talks or after one of our training sessions, but none had ever said it that way. The words profound impact seemed to give a new sense of responsibility to what I do.

I also remember sitting there feeling a little embarrassed. It wasn't false humility. Without sounding arrogant, I'm good at what I do. I know that one of the gifts God gave me is the ability to persuade others and to communicate effectively. Every time I give a talk or teach a session of any kind, I sincerely hope and believe what I say makes a difference – that people in my audiences get some relief from their day to day worries, when they laugh at my stories; that they reflect on their lives and renew their commitment to make this a better world, when I share stories that illustrate my philosophy of life. I always want to have an impact and it would be wonderful, if it were profound. She was just the first to ever put those two words together.

She went on to tell me how her husband had carried that copy of the poem I'd given him three years earlier at a meeting of the Virginia Automobile Dealers Association - how he had carried it with him every day right up to his death and had tried to emulate all I had shared in my talk to them at The Greenbriar Hotel. She told me several other things about the kind of man her husband had been and how he had lived his life. She then told me that since the poem had meant so much to her husband, would I please send one copy for each of her four children. By that point, I would have sent her a case of poems. I did send her what she had requested, plus, I sent back the copy her husband had carried for three years, because I know how much items once belonging to my Daddy mean to me, and I felt that one of their sons would like to have the very same copy his Dad had carried.

Her impassioned letter was also a serious reminder of the responsibility I have to my audiences in both the public and private sectors of life. Each of us is an example, whether positive or negative, to those around us. Whether we like it or not, people are always examining our responses to life. But that's another chapter...in fact, it's the next one.

CHAPTER 7

BIG AUTHENTICITY

"There are three things extremely hard: steel, a diamond, and to know one's self".

Ben Franklin

When I started writing this chapter, I sat there in front of my keyboard thinking about one of the belts I wear. It has a stamp on it that says, "Genuine Leather." That is authenticity. When we see the word "genuine" we know it is the real thing . . . it is authentic. It isn't any more or any less. . . . just the real thing. What you see is what you get. The real thing usually has a higher value; it costs more than the fake stuff. Furniture laminated with a simulated wood grain is a lot less expensive than a solid piece of furniture with real wood grain. Real cotton or silk usually costs more than synthetics. And I'll take real strawberries over strawberry flavoring any day of the week, won't you?

All of this applies double to people. My closest friends are the real deal. I know they aren't busy trying to impress me. They aren't running around showing off. They really are what they say they are. They live a life that demonstrates that they really are who they say they are.

I continued to learn that lesson as a little (ok, so I was never really little) as a young boy. My daddy was an ardent camper. Between daddy and scouts I spent a lot of time in the woods. Every summer Daddy took our family camping somewhere. We would often go to Smokemont, a campground in the Smokey Mountains of North Carolina, or maybe some other campground in Tennessee, or Virginia, or in our home state of South Carolina. Wherever we went, though, my sister Anne and my brothers Tim and Wes, could usually count on a visit to the Cherokee Indian Reservation in Cherokee, North Carolina.

We seemed to always have an accumulation of Indian gear that we had picked up along the way. We had tomahawks with the painted handles, war bonnets with lots of feathers, tom-toms that were tied down with rawhide (those seemed to disappear quite often. I think Mama was periodically hiding them somewhere), deadly spears with genuine rubber tips, and a real leather whip. Lash LaRue was a hero of mine back then. He was a cowboy, dressed all in black, and never carried a gun, only a whip. I learned to make the sound of a whip snapping and can do it to this day. I also remember defoliating most of the shrubbery with my whip before my parents stopped me. In addition to all that, I could always count on my ever present bow and arrows. The only problem was that the only kind of bow and arrow set my dad would let me have was the kind that had that rubber suction cup on it. You know, the kind you had to lick before you could get it to stick on anything.

One year, when I was about ten years old, I talked Daddy into buying me a real bow and arrow. No suction cup stuff. The bow was one of those stout bows you had to bend a little to attach the string and the arrows were target arrows. They had a metal tip that came to a point, but since they were target arrows, they were a little blunt. They were long and had the little feathers at the end, and, of course, they were painted with different colors of war paint.

I couldn't wait to get home and try them out. As soon as we hit the driveway, I jumped out and started putting up targets all over the yard. I had little pieces of paper and cardboard scattered everywhere. I spent hours out there practicing, and after a few weeks, I was getting pretty good. I was hitting within 8 to 10 feet of anything I was trying to shoot.

One Saturday morning, Mother and Daddy had gone shopping and had left me in charge of everything. Three of my buddies, Larry Kendall, Mike Mills and Stuart Thompson, were over at the house and I decided I wanted to impress them with my new found skills with the bow. I decided that what would really impress these guys and put me at the top of the pecking order in our little neighborhood group, would be to kill something. So, I looked around for something to kill. I couldn't find anything until I came up with the positively brilliant idea to use my sister for a target. I went in the house and talked Anne into coming out in the yard. I'd already heard about William Tell and the apple on the head story. I thought about that, but decided against it. I think what prompted my getting Anne is that it seemed to me that every other Sunday night on The Ed Sullivan Show (or "shoe", as he said it), one of the more popular acts was when a couple would come on stage dressed in some gypsy looking outfits. The man would tie the woman to a huge wooden wheel and start her spinning slowly. Then he would walk abut 15 feet back and someone would blindfold him. After he was successfully blindfolded, a drum roll would begin and he would very dramatically throw knives at her and perfectly outline her body with them.

I'm thinking I could do the same thing with a bow and arrow. Luckily for Anne, there wasn't a wheel to be found anywhere in the neighborhood. So, I had her stand with her feet as far apart as she could get them and I planned to shoot each arrow in succession into the ground between her feet.

She stood there very still trusting her older brother. I took fifteen paces back and with my three buddies lined up behind me, reached back into my quiver and pulled out the first arrow. I took dead aim right inside her right foot and let the arrow fly. Right at the last moment a little shift in the wind pulled the arrow off course, and it ended up hitting her right above her left knee.

At that exact moment, Mama and Daddy pulled up in the driveway from buying groceries. The scene they saw unfold before their very eyes, as they topped the little hill headed to our house, must have seemed surreal to them. They had to have thought, "surely our oldest son is not planning to kill our only daughter" and if they did, they were right. I really did not want to kill her, I just wanted to use her as a target.

Daddy gunned the car into the driveway. Both front doors flew open. Mother ran to Anne hollering and screaming, and Daddy came flying around the back end of the car headed straight toward me. Chaos was beginning to break out all around me. I remember looking up at my Daddy and thinking, "I'm probably in a little bit of trouble here." My "fight or flight" instincts began to kick in and I knew running away from him could be fatal. So I just stood there, frozen in place. As he got closer to me, it seemed like everything went into slow motion, like we've all seen in the movies. I also remember thinking, "so this is what <u>death</u> looks like when it's coming right at you." About half way to me, he reached down and started unbuckling his belt and ripping it off as he ran. I don't know if you were raised under the leather like I was or not, but if you were, you know exactly what that looks like and the sound it makes as the end of the belt hit each loop of his pants on it's way out.

I looked around for some support from my buddies, but they were gone. When <u>their</u> fight or flight stimuli kicked in, they took off, leaving me to fight this monster all by myself.

We found out later that if Anne had simply opened her hand, the arrow would have simply fallen to the ground, and she could have turned and walked back into the house like a normal human being, because the arrow was not stuck in her leg. It had just barely punctured the skin, but she had a death grip on it. Could she have let go and just walk away, thus saving her older brothers neck? Oh no. She held onto the arrow and backed herself into the house, dragging her leg and looking to me a lot like Festus on the old Gunsmoke TV show. Remember? "I'm coming, Mr. Dillon, I'm coming," as he limped along.

I knew as this whole thing unfolded that she wasn't hurt, because as she hobbled up the steps and started into the house through the front door, she glanced back at me with a devilish little grin and a look that only a sibling would understand. It was a look that said, "I gotcha now," and she played it all the way out. Meanwhile, Daddy was breaking up my bow and arrows, while he was simultaneously wearing my rear end out with his belt.

Years later when our family sat around telling family stories, everybody would laugh when the arrow story was retold - everybody, but Daddy. He never saw any humor in that story at all. Now as an adult with two daughters, I understand why. He had three sons and one daughter. He could have given up one of us boys, but not his little girl.

That is my first memory of how showing off, trying to be something you aren't, and doing something you shouldn't be doing in the first place, can get you in trouble. I wish I could tell you that was all I needed to completely learn that lesson, but I wouldn't be honest if I did. It took me a few more times to learn to just be me and to try to be the very best _me_ I could possibly be.

I believe that anyone who is going about the business of being themselves _has_ and _shows_ more confidence. Not arrogance, but confidence. One way I've always liked to look at confidence is that it is a healthy belief in oneself to the point of arrogance with a BIG dose of humility.

Early in my speaking career, my good friend Bill Ferguson asked me to speak for Kanawah Insurance Company, when he was Vice President of Sales. The meeting was held in New Orleans, Louisiana, and was an awards trip for the salespeople who had met their quotas. Bill wanted me to speak at a luncheon for only about thirty minutes, and he wanted the talk to be primarily humorous with a little bit of a message.

The audience was one of the best I have ever had. They laughed and laughed and laughed some more. It seemed like everything I said was more than just funny. It was, as we've sometimes called it, "drop dead funny." When I finished my talk, several of them came up to me and went on and on about how much they had enjoyed the talk, how funny I was, and how they couldn't wait to hear me again.

I floated out of the luncheon with "the big head" as I went back to my room to get my bags, catch a taxi, and head to the airport for my next flight. After I got my bags, I decided to take the long way to the lobby, because it would take me by the rooms where Bill and his folks from Kanawah were having other meetings. I thought maybe I could troll for some more comments about how wonderful I was. How's that for arrogance?

I am convinced that what happened next was God's way of helping me come down from arrogance to confidence. As I slowly strolled by the meeting rooms, a little elderly lady, about five feet tall with gray hair, came up to me and said, "Mr. Walker, I couldn't get to you after the luncheon because there were so many people around you (can't you just see my head getting bigger and bigger), but I wanted to tell you that you are the greatest professional speaker I have ever heard. Truth is, though, you are the <u>only</u> professional speaker I've ever heard."

I couldn't help but laugh at her comment. . . and at my puffery. That comment, from what I honestly believe was an Angel sent from Heaven, brought me back down to earth and I was able to get my head out the front door of the hotel and on my way to the airport and my next speech with confidence, not arrogance.

Some of my greatest lessons have come from children. My daughter Amy has taught me several. A young fellow reinforced one as we were leaving a University of South Carolina football game with several thousand other people. On the way down the exit ramps, filled with thousands of people moving, elbow to elbow, moving like an army of ants down the concrete incline, I heard a man's voice behind me yell out, "Son, let's don't get lost now." A young fellow, not more than ten or twelve years old walking down in front of us, whipped around and yelled back up at his daddy, "We won't if y'all will keep up with me." The little guy was confident. He knew exactly what he was doing and where he was going.

I remember chuckling to myself when that happened. For some reason, the incident stuck with me, and I realized there is a great lesson for all of us wrapped up in that exchange between a Father and his son. I remember hearing the man behind me tell his wife, or whoever he was with, "He'll be ok. He knows where the car is."

That comment reminded me that when we have a clear focus, we know exactly what we have to do and how to get where we are headed. We can step out sharply, just like that boy did. My most frustrating times as an adult have been when I was shooting at so many targets that none of them were in focus. We all know we can hit more with a shotgun, but the majority of experts in target shooting use a rifle. One shot, aimed skillfully, has a lot better chance of success than a spray of shots aimed in the general direction of the target.

Here's another lesson from a child about confidence. You may have heard the story of the little young girl who was playing with some crayons and her Mother asked her what she was drawing. "A picture of God," said the little girl. "Nobody knows what God looks like," replied the Mother. The little girt didn't even look up from her work. She kept right on coloring, as she told her Mother, "They will when I get through!" That is confidence.

Our daughter Janna has a son, our grandson. His name is Madison and when he was a little over 4 years old, she was having trouble getting him to go to bed and go to sleep. One particular evening she'd gotten him to bed and she heard him playing with some of his toys. "Get back in bed, Madison." "Yes, ma'am." Then she heard him flipping pages in a book. "Put the book up and go to sleep." "Yes, ma'am." A few seconds went by. "I need some water." "You've already had water. Go to sleep." A few more seconds later, "I need to go to the bathroom." "You've already gone to the bathroom. Now go to sleep." Janna said she could almost hear him thinking about what he could come up with next.

Then she heard, "Prayers – we haven't said our prayers." She couldn't say no to that and went into his room, knelt down by the bed with him, and said her prayer. At the time, Janna was working on buying her first house, so some of her prayers were that if God meant for it to be, that everything would work out on her loan and with the contractor. When she finished, Madison said, "My turn." Then he sternly said, "God, we got to have a house and we got to have it right now." Janna interrupted him and told him that we didn't talk to God in that tone. Madison got a little more humble and said very softly, "I'm sorry, God. Could we please have a house?" The next thing Janna heard was Madison saying out of the corner of his mouth, "Sure." Then she heard, "Well, can I have some candy?" And again, "Sure." By this time she's about to bite a hole in her lip to keep from laughing and Madison continues to ask for a few more things, each time turning away from his mama and out of the corner of his mouth, in a lower voice saying, "Sure." Finally, he ends his prayer with, "Thank you, God, and Amen." The last thing Janna heard before she exploded was, "You're welcome, Madison." I either have a grandson who is one heck of a ventriloquist or he thinks he is God. Now, how's that for confidence!

Early on in my career their were a couple of speakers that I really admired and wanted to emulate – Zig Ziglar, Robert Henry, Jeanne Robertson, Nido Qubein, Ty Boyd and others, but I couldn't get down on one knee like Zig, I wasn't from a home town that had a name I could drag out like Robert could, when he'd say Aubuuuuuuuuuuuurn, Alabama, I had never been a "Miss Anything" like Jeanne, even though I have an accent, it's not like that of my friend Nido, and I could never have the broadcaster's voice of Ty. God had already made one of each of them and, no matter how hard I might try, I could never <u>be</u> them.

Two of the most authentic and godly people I know are our dear friends, Chuck and Bonnie Ferrell. They own a BBQ restaurant and a couple of chicken restaurants in Auburn and Opelika, Alabama and serve some of the best food this side of heave. Every time I think of authenticity, I think of them. They proven they can be successful, but more importantly, they've proven their humility and their dependence on God, time and time again. They are truly the real deal...to the core.

Thank goodness I figured out early on in my career, that what I could be was the best Al Walker possible and nobody else could ever <u>be</u> me. That's one of the reasons I don't mind sharing my best stories with the world, because no one can tell them like I can, since they happened to me and me alone. Plus, if someone else ever tells me that they heard such and such a speaker tell the same story, I can whip out my book and show them the truth.

Confidence and authenticity go together. Point: Don't waste time and energy trying to impress people by trying to be something or someone you're not. Just work on becoming whatever it is you want to be. The rest of the world will know when you get there.

CHAPTER 8

BIG LOVE

"IF YOU DON'T LOVE YOURSELF, THAT PROBABLY MAKES IT UNANIMOUS."

The happiest people I know love themselves, the people around them, and they love what they do. I don't mean this in some narcissistic sort of way. They like who they are and are comfortable with themselves. You can tell by the smiles on their faces, their energy, and their attention to and concern for others that they feel good about who they are. They sincerely love other people and look for ways to show it through a special note, an encouraging comment, or a hug right when it is needed the most.

Several years ago I was conducting a workshop in Greenville, South Carolina, and a friend of mine, Judy Jones Cannon, currently, the head of Alumnae affairs at Columbia College, was in the session. We had a chance to visit a little when it was over. During our conversation, Judy asked me if I had seen our friend Charlie Farrell lately. I told her that I hadn't, but that it was interesting she asked about Charlie, because I was going to see him that night at a Columbia Chamber of Commerce banquet being held at the Officers Club at Fort Jackson.

"Would you do me a favor?" she asked. I nodded yes and then she asked if I would give Charlie a hug from her when I saw him. I told her I would be glad to, but that we would have to hug again, because I wasn't going to give Charlie the hug I had gotten from her earlier. We laughed, hugged, and I headed on back to Columbia.

When I walked into the Officers Club that evening, I immediately spotted Charlie way across the room. I remembered my assignment and walked right over to him to tell him about seeing Judy and to deliver her hug. As I approached him, he saw me and I said, "Charlie, I saw a friend of ours today, Judy Cannon, and she told me to give you a hug for her when I saw you," and I stuck out my arms to hug Charlie.

Charlie took a step backwards and said, "Whoa. Wait a minute. Calm yourself. I don't want you hugging me in front of all these people." There was a young lady standing next to Charlie whom I had never seen before in my life. I had no idea who she was, but Charlie turned to her and asked, "Would you do us a favor? Would you let us pass the hug through you?" "Sure," she said and she and I hugged. I didn't want to cheat Charlie out of his entire hug from Judy, so I hugged this woman real good. I'm talking an industrial strength, BIG TIME hug. When we finished, she turned to Charlie and gave him the hug. Charlie, wanting to make sure he got all of Judy's hug, also demonstrated his hugging adeptness.

During the hug, Charlie looked at me with that "light bulb" look that told me he'd just had an idea and I knew we were having the exact same thought. The rest of the night, if he saw me standing with someone he wanted to hug, or if I saw him standing with someone I wanted to hug, one of us would walk up to the other one and start with, "Saw a friend of yours today. . ."

We pulled that little scam until I honestly believe we hugged every woman in that room before the night was over. Charlie and I have talked about that several times over the years and I have told that story in many a speech. Charlie has even had people, who have previously heard me speak, come up to him after one of his talks and ask him if that story is true. Charlie and I both agree that we don't need gimmicks like that to let other people know we care about them.

People who love BIG TIME and in a BIG WAY look for ways to show others that they care. There are so many things you can do to express your concern for others that don't have to cost very much money and can still have a BIG impact. Examples include a note left in any number of places...a sock drawer, where she keeps her make-up, in a desk drawer, or tucked away in a suitcase where it will be found when the suitcase is opened later - like the love notes I find from my wife that mean so much when I open my suitcase two thousand miles from her and our home. How about going down twenty or thirty pages in someone's note pad, or post it note pad, and writing a thank you note to an associate? Here's something special that someone once did that didn't cost him a dime.

When I was just five or six years old, my Daddy came to me a few days before my birthday and said he had a special surprise for me for my birthday. My birthday fell on a Saturday that year and he told me he had a real treat planned. He told me to get my buddies together and be in the car first thing Saturday morning.

When Saturday morning arrived, my parents, my sister Anne, and three of my best buddies, Larry Kendall, Stuart Thompson, and Bruce Smith all piled in the car and we headed downtown. On the way, Daddy announced that he had arranged for a parade in honor of my birthday. WOW!!! A parade for me? What a great surprise! None of us could believe it. We lit up with excitement, and sure enough, as Daddy pulled our car into a parking space right in front of J.C. Penny's department store in downtown Columbia, the crowd was already gathering.

Daddy told us to sit on the trunk lid and that everybody would wave at us. I was placed in the seat of honor, right in the middle of the pack. With my buddies around me, shocked that my dad was having a parade for me, I could not have felt more alive. We waved to the people who lined the parade route, and, sure enough, they waved back!

Then the parade started and the dignitaries and the beauty queens all came by sitting in cars or on the backs of convertibles. They all looked directly at me and waved. I could see them mouthing the words, "Happy Birthday, Albert," as they rode by.

Then came my favorite parts - the bands, the clowns, and the soldiers with flags flapping in the breeze. To this day, I still get chills up and down my spine when I see soldiers or cadets in uniforms, marching to the strong sound of a band, being led by a color guard with Old Glory and a battalion or regimental flag with battle and honor ribbons flying proudly in the air.

This parade was the best ever. It not only had all the bands, but it had a lot of soldiers, jeeps, and tanks from Fort Jackson, as well as, representatives from all the other branches of service. I didn't learn till a few years later that my Daddy had brought us to the annual Armed Forces Day parade that just happened to fall on the same day as my birthday that year.

It didn't matter, though. Even when I found out the parade hadn't been for me and that all the other people didn't know they were there to celebrate my birthday. All I remember thinking, then and now, is how my Daddy loved me enough to make that particular Saturday, May the 19th, so special for me, his son. It didn't cost him any money. He didn't have to go to a lot of trouble. He just had to be sharp enough and love me enough to always be on the look out for things he could do to make me feel like the special human being he always told me I was.

That is BIG TIME love - when we love someone enough to always be on the lookout for how we can make them feel like the special and unique people they are. When was the last time you made someone feel special?

Love to me also means having a passion for what you do. My wife Margaret is a schoolteacher. She love's what she does. When we were married, we agreed that she would quit teaching and travel around the country with me. She did that for the first two years we were married and I wouldn't take anything for that time we had together.

Yet, the tug of teaching kept pulling at her. One day she was reading the paper and noticing all the ads for teachers. She looked up at me and said she wanted to go back to teaching. She had her Master's degree plus 30 and right at 20 years teaching experience. I left it up to her.

When I returned from one of my speaking trips, she announced she had an interview for a teaching position at one of the local high schools. There are 4 or 5 high schools within reasonable driving distance from our home, so I asked her, "which one?" "Birchwood," she said. I started chuckling, "You don't know where Birchwood is, do you?" "No, but I'm sure I can find it," she replied.

I then went on to tell her that it was the high school at the Department of Juvenile Justice and that I didn't want her teaching there. She said, "Well, you know they asked me if I'd ever taught any criminals before and I said of course. I taught public high school for almost 20 years. I imagine I must have had a few in some of my classes. I didn't know she meant *all* of them."

She <u>went</u> for the interview, took the job, and is still as excited and as passionate today about teaching as I'm sure she was when she first started. She LOVES teaching in a BIG way. And I know her students appreciate what she does for them. Just the other day one of them said to her, "You're running G, on me, but you know what time it is."

Just in case you don't know prison jargon, what that means is he felt like she was running a game on him...manipulating him to do something he really didn't want to do, but that it was ok, because she was doing it for the right reasons and that she was an ok person.

The most appropriate way I can end this chapter is to tell you about a man who had such a BIG, loving spirit that the highest award given by The National Speakers Association is a bronze statue of the man himself who inspired it. The award is called The Cavett and stands proudly in my office today. Cavett Robert is one of my heroes.

Cavett didn't start speaking professionally until he was sixty years old and spoke until his death in 1997. Cavett was born in Mississippi, became an attorney, practiced law in New York and moved to Arizona where the doctors told him he needed to be for health reasons. Even though Cavett, along with Merlyn Cundiff, founded The National Speakers Association, which today has approximately 3,500 members and is the voice of the speaking profession, the smartest thing he ever did was marry his wonderful wife Trudy who was the first Miss South Carolina. Trudy will always be the first lady of NSA.

Cavett had a little poem he used in almost every one of his talks that is the secret to BIG love. I want to share it with you as a gift from Cavett to you.

A bell's not a bell, till you ring it.

A song's not a song, till you sing it.

Love wasn't put in your heart to stay.

Love isn't love till you give it away.

I'm sure Cavett would echo my encouragement to you to love yourself. Be proud of who you are – a unique creation of God; to love your family, friends and the folks you work with (as hard as that might be sometimes); and love what you do. Life is just too short to do otherwise.

CHAPTER 9

A BIG SENSE OF HUMOR

"Laughter is God's hands on the shoulders of a troubled world."
Minnie Pearl.

We were all taught the five senses when we were in school – taste, touch, hearing, sight, and smell. We also know about that sixth sense that some people refer to as their gut reaction. I believe we have a seventh sense that is as God given as the other six. We call it a sense of humor. I honestly believe everybody has one; some just haven't used theirs in a loooooooong time.

If you are the kind of person who loves to laugh and loves to see others laugh, you know what a wonderful gift you've been given. If you would like to develop your gift a little more, I have three suggestions:

♦ Be observant – funny things are happening all around you.
♦ Say the funny stuff that comes to your mind.
♦ Hang out with funny people.

Being more observant means accepting the fact that funny stuff does happen all around you every day. You may have just said to yourself, "not around me." I disagree. I believe it does happen all around us and some of us just need to pay better attention.

For instance, one morning, my wife Margaret and I were standing in front of our bathroom mirror getting ready to go to work and I was spraying some volumizing gel in my hair. She asked, "what's that?" I told her and then added, "I just need more body." She didn't say a word. She just looked at me and started laughing. I did, too, when I realized how that must have sounded coming out of the mouth of a 375 pound man.

On the way to church one Sunday morning, I pulled out a CD I had not listened to in years and could not remember what the group sounded like. I told my wife I'd found a CD of Gospel music I wanted her to hear. When I told her it was by a group called The Five Blind Boys From Alabama, she asked, "How'd they find each other?"

As I was writing this book early one morning, my wonderful wife kept interrupting me with one thought after another. After about the third or fourth comment from her, I was getting perturbed and asked, "You reckon anyone kept interrupting Ernest Hemingway while he was writing?" She said, "Yes, and that's probably why he committed suicide. So, if I can just make it look like an accident, I'll be in business!" She, of course, was referring to the Million Dollar accidental death policy we have on my life. Veeerrry funny!

Margaret also has a loving sense of humor. She has had many an opportunity to make fun of me or come back at me after I just made some inane comment. Like the time we were staying in a two-story mountain house in the Smokey Mountains – Pigeon Forge, to be exact. We were there to attend a Gaither Family Fest Concert in Gatlinburg, Tennessee. Our bedroom was upstairs and one wall was entirely glass, which gave us an incredible view of the mountains. When we woke up the first morning, I raised up on one elbow and said, "Aren't the mountains in this part of western North Carolina just beautiful?" "Honey," she said so sweetly, "I think they call this part of North Carolina, Tennessee." We both started laughing. Yes, our life together could be one big sit – com. It's not enough to be more observant, you must write it down, if you want to remember it later. Get a copy of my friend Jeanne Robertson's book, <u>Don't Let The Funny Stuff Get Away</u> and do what it says. You can find her at www.jeannerobertson.com. That book has helped me keep up with the funny stuff I run across every day in airports, cabs, at the office, at home, and just about everywhere I go.

The second idea as to how you can better use your God given gift is to say the funny stuff when you think of it. Just blurt it on right out there - not if it's mean or cutting or sarcastic...but genuinely funny.

My buddy Kurt Kilpatrick often quotes Will Rogers who said, "if there ain't no malice in your heart, there can't be none in your jokes."

One of the funniest people I know on the planet is a friend of mine right in my hometown. We grew up together and he has always been able to make me and everyone else around him laugh. Extremely and creatively bright, he mostly just says whatever thought just came to his mind. Everyone knows he makes up, at least, half the stuff he tells us, but it's ok because it is always funny. His name is Robert "Bullet" Bass, the son of Bob "The Hawk" Bass (who got his nickname from his big ole hawk like beak of a nose that probably got that way from his football playing days at The University of North Carolina) and Mrs. Margie "Always Has A Smile On Her Face And Can Make You Feel Like You Are The Most Important Person In The World" Bass.

Robert got his nickname from his days as a young athlete when he could run like the wind. Truth is, he looked faster than he really was, but he was "fleet of foot" and faster than most, a good football and baseball player, and thoroughly enjoyed a challenge of almost any kind.

I could write a book about our experiences that are such a rich part of our lives; from when we shot at each other with BB guns, to the many times we went camping with Terry and Dennis Easler, to our adolescent and young adult days spent at Myrtle Beach. I won't bore you with all of them, but here's one quick Myrtle Beach story that shows Robert's BIG thinking.

One of the great traditions in South Carolina is called "First week." It is always the first week after the end of the school year. From about the 10th or 11th grade in high school on through college we made our annual trek to the Grand Strand that first week in June. All the high school age people stayed down around Myrtle Beach and the college age people stayed at Ocean Drive. So, when we graduated from high school, we also graduated from Myrtle Beach and headed up to Ocean Drive and the now enshrined "Pad," which was a little hole in the wall that had every shag song you'd ever heard on the juke box from Sixty Minute Man and The White Cliffs of Dover to every song the Tams, Drifter, Temptations, and many others ever recorded. Pat Conroy even wrote a book called Beach Music that included this annual ritual.

One year when we were in high school in the mid 1960's, we stayed at a little duplex in Myrtle Beach with, at least, 6 or 8 other guys. Robert and I had walked downtown toward the pavilion and came up on the Gay Dolphin, a landmark gift shop that is still standing today and was named back when gay just meant happy.

In front of the Gay Dolphin stood a steel box about four feet high and a foot to a foot and a half square. Standing on top of this steel pedestal was a 10-inch high man made out of several pieces of steel with movable joints. He was skewered onto a steel rod that came up out of the pedestal and he was positioned on the rod so that his feet barely touched the top of the pedestal. There was a slot on the front of the pedestal where you could put in a dime, and as soon as the dime got to its destination, the machine would crank up. A high-spirited song with a quick rhythm would then start from somewhere inside the box. The medal rod would start moving up and down and shaking back and forth, and the little mechanical metal man would start dancing. His feet and arms would be moving in every direction and since his little feet were metal on metal, it sounded like he was tap dancing at a frantic pace no human could match. It also had a sign on all sides calling this thing "The Dancing Fool."

Well, it didn't take us long to draw a crowd because every time I put a dime in the box and The Dancing Fool cranked up, Robert "Mr. I Love A BIG Crowd" Bass would imitate The Dancing Fool. No, he would become The Dancing Fool. People would stand there just howling with laughter, and it wasn't long before they started putting dimes in the machine themselves when it stopped, because it would only go for about a minute for 10 cents. They wanted more of both dancing fools. . .the machine and Robert.

Another one of my funny friends is my speaker buddy Ralph Hood. Ralph is a very funny man. He is a Clemson graduate and I guess having a sense of humor helped him get through Clemson. He's also a member of Mensa, which, as you probably know, is the organization to which you pay $400, so they can validate that you are smart and Ralph is. He writes a syndicated column that is carried by a number of newspapers. He is also an aviator and writes for several aviation periodicals.

My gall bladder was removed in 1992, following one of the diets I wrote about in the first chapter. I had to be in the hospital for a couple of days, because laparoscopic surgery had not worked for me and they had to cut me from stem to stern to get my gall bladder out. When I got home a few days later, my answering machine light was telling me that I had a message. As it turned out, I had several, but I never will forget the first one. It was from Ralph, who is also a big guy like I am. "Al, I hear you been sick. I hope you get better, but if you don't make it, can I have your suits?" I tried not to laugh, cause it hurt, but I couldn't help it. I just burst out.

My dear friend and partner in Platform Professionals, Doc Blakely from Wharton, Texas, tells the story about one particular flight he had into Chicago's O'Hare International Airport on Delta Airlines. Doc said the plane landed abruptly and jarred all the passengers. Since 80% of the people on any airplane do not fly a lot, any thing that seems out of sorts scares them to death. Doc told me that when the plane hit the runway as hard as it did, you could tell it scared most of his fellow passengers. The flight attendant, realizing she had a plane full of frightened people, took it into her own hands to use her God given sense of humor. She grabbed the intercom and announced, "Ladies and Gentlemen, we have just attacked Chicago and they have surrendered!" Doc said laughter erupted and you could feel all the tension dissipate immediately. Her quick thinking and use of her sense of humor made for some BIG relief for her passengers.

Humor is one of the best stress relievers known to man. If you can see something funny in even difficult or challenging situations, it helps you stay calmer, stimulates your creativity, and enables you to have a better view of the situation.

I was on a Delta flight one Sunday evening flying to Ft. Lauderdale. I was doing a series of programs for Arvida Realty that started first thing Monday morning. I was sitting in seat 1B on a

Boeing 747 and my seat mate in 1A was an off duty flight attendant headed home. Row one in first class is directly opposite the galley in a 747. The flight attendants' seat is on the cabin side of the cockpit wall and folds up out of the way when not in use. Between the flight attendants' seat and row one is a double closet that opens to the aisle.

The flight attendant, who is facing coach when seated, can clearly see the person seated in 1B, which on <u>this</u> flight was me. As we lifted off we all heard a fairly loud sound that sounded like air rushing either in or out, literally "a giant sucking sound." The service door for the first class galley was directly across the aisle from me on the other wall of the plane. It has a 4 or 5 inch wide strip of rubber that helps seal the door when it is closed.

The sound got louder and my seat mate and I realized the rubber gasket on the door was slowly moving out, as if the door would eventually be sucked out of the opening. Wanting to utilize some humor to help relieve the stress, I turned to her with my almost 400lb. body and said, "If the door goes, I'll just throw myself over the opening and y'all can just stack up behind me." She laughed a little nervously. Then we both agreed that if it moved much further, we were headed to the back of the plane.

I signaled to the flight attendant facing me that the door was not completely closed and that was where the noise was coming from. She grabbed her telephone, said something to the pilot, and the plane immediately leveled off from it's steep climb, made a hard circle around to the right, dumped fuel (probably in Lake Lanier), and landed back at Hartsfield International. We taxied back to the gate and someone got on the plane and secured the door. We found out that a Marriott food caterer had managed to turn the lock on the door <u>before</u> it was completely closed. We also found out that he was fired on the spot for endangering a plane full of people.

Everybody who knows me, knows that my two best friends in the world outside of my wife and family are both named Robert. Robert Henry, my dear friend from Auburn, Alabama, who passed away in September, 2001, his wife Merrilyn, their two boys, Brent and Patrick, and my daughter, Amy, and I went on a fabulous vacation in

1986. Along with about 30 other speaker friends, we went on a seven day, six night raft ride down the Colorado River through the Grand Canyon. It was spectacular!

Each night when we pulled in to our campsite, we formed lines from the boats to the shore and unloaded our gear. We unloaded cooking gear, food, our duffel bags, and the cots and sleeping bags we used instead of tents. Every night was clear and I'll never forget sleeping out under the stars, all warm and cozy in my sleeping bag. All of us went to bed each night on our cots, except for one couple...Virgil Beasley and his wife.

They had brought a small pop up tent along and would set it up in the middle of our campsite. One day Robert and I were walking by the tent, probably on our way to get something to eat, when both of us saw Virgil's wife changing clothes. I mean, you could see right through the netting and there she was in broad daylight. . .changing clothes.

We saw Virgil a few minutes later and my funny friend Robert said to him, "Virgil, I know something your wife thinks." "What? asked Virgil. "She thinks nobody can see inside y'all's tent when she's changing clothes." We all got a good laugh and Robert made his point without hurting anybody's feelings.

Two people whom I admire a lot are Jerry and Jackie Yarborough. They have two wonderful children named Jennifer and Ernie...both of whom are adults and married. Jennifer and her husband Bob live in Charleston, SC, with their children. Ernie and his wife Nichole and their child live in Columbia. Jerry has said for years he has spent his entire life being known as either Cale Yarborough's brother or Ernie Yarborough's dad. Truth is, Jerry is well known for the tremendous success he has had in business. He is one of the top Nationwide Insurance Agents in the country and has garnered the respect and admiration of everyone in Columbia who knows him.

A few years ago, Jerry decided to get back into flying. He had obtained his private pilot's license back in the early nineteen sixty's, but had not flown in some time. When he decided to pick it back up, he had to go back through the same process as someone who was new to flying. After meeting all the requirements on the ground and with his instructor, Jerry had to then plan a cross-country trip, in order to get his private pilot's license. That is a requirement for all flight students. I guess, if you plan your trip, take it, and get back alive that means you're a pilot.

Jerry's planned trip took him from Columbia's Owens Field to Myrtle Beach to Charleston and back. Each time he had to land, get his logbook signed, get back in his plane, and fly to his next destination. On the first leg from Columbia to Myrtle Beach, SC, Jerry's line of flight took him right over McIntire Field, which is South Carolina's Air National Guard Base. He crossed their air space without any difficulty and with little recognition.

As soon as he left McIntire's air space, he entered the air space of another military base: Shaw Field, which is a U.S. Air Force base located in Sumter, SC. As soon as he hit their air space, a voice came over his radio. "You have entered the area of a government military facility and we have you on our radar. You have permission to cross our air space, but please hurry on through, because we have 4 F-16's scheduled to take off in less than sixty seconds."

Jerry, using his God given sense of humor said to the U.S. Air Force, "Send 'em on up here. I'll give 'em a flying lesson!" The folks in the tower immediately came back with, "What kind of airplane are you flying and what is the horsepower?" Jerry proudly told them he was flying a Cherokee 160 which, just in case you might not know, is a single engine, four seater, with a 150 horsepower engine that might be able to push that little plane along at an air speed of maybe - just maybe, 100 miles an hour, if it had a strong tail wind.

As soon as Jerry told him what he was flying, a chuckle came from the tower and a few seconds later they came back and said, "We've discussed it among ourselves and we've decided it's a negatory on the flying lessons. We feel a little outclassed." Jerry then went on to tell me how he saw those four F-16's take off as he was flying overhead. He told me what a magnificent sight that was to watch those powerful planes with fire shooting out the back to go screaming down the runway and take off.

Jerry said he headed on toward Myrtle Beach to the first stop of his cross country flight and didn't think anymore about the good laugh they had all just enjoyed. In about fifteen minutes, two F-16's showed up on each side of Jerry's little ole airplane. They were standing almost straight up, flying almost on their tails, so they could slow up enough for Jerry to see them as they went by. "I tried to ignore 'em," Jerry said.

Since Jerry told me that story, I have had a mental image of those three planes flying side-by-side. Jerry and his plane flying horizontal and the two war planes on each side of him flying along almost vertical. Here we have two U.S. Air Force fighter jets that cost, at least, a gazillion dollars apiece. The helmets alone that the pilots were wearing probably cost $10,000 a piece. Then, here sits Jerry in his 4 seater, single engine with it's one little propeller turning. Jerry with a NASCAR tee shirt on, a baseball cap turned around 'backards', and probably a Coke or a Pepsi with some peanuts in it sitting on the seat beside him (the only way I thought you could drink a coke when I was growing up). Jerry said that after a few seconds of his trying to act like they weren't there, he glanced over at both pilots and they had their visors back, were grinning from ear to ear, and both gave him a thumbs up. Jerry just grinned, threw his head back, and acted like he was flying an F-16 with 'em.

Jerry couldn't wait to come to the office the next Monday, after having had this experience on Saturday, so he could tell me all about it. He knows how much I love a good laugh and, more importantly how much I appreciate hearing how someone saw the opportunity to grab a chunk of life and used their God given sense of humor to help themselves and the others around them have an above average moment. I've wondered how many other pilots of small air planes, flying over Shaw Air Force Base have had that same opportunity and didn't take it.

Why don't more people see the laughter in life? Here's my take on that. They are too busy putting a lot more importance on themselves than they should. In other words, they are simply taking themselves too seriously. Lighten up. Life is just too short to get so bogged down and caught up in the small stuff that you miss the fun stuff.

Speaking of small stuff, one of the most sincere, genuine, and "other centered" couples I know are Ray and Rosita Perez, who live in Gainesville, Florida. They both came to America from Cuba as young children and had wonderful careers. Ray was a DEA (Drug Enforcement Agent) and Rosita was a social worker turned Professional Speaker. She has always had a flower in her hair, a song on her lips, and love and compassion in her heart for everyone she meets.

As Ray tells it, whenever anything would happen and Ray would make a concerned comment about it, invariably, Rosita would say, "Don't sweat the small stuff." Ray said that he'd heard her say that time and time again to the point that one day he asked her to tell him the difference between small stuff and big stuff.

She said, "That's easy. First, here's the big stuff. You're born - you die. That's BIG stuff. Everything else in between? That's small stuff." He smiled when he told me that and said, "Now I got it." And they both really do go through life not sweating the small stuff.

Shouldn't we do the same? Having that attitude doesn't mean you become flippant about the important issues of life. You still have to pay your bills, do what you say you're going to do and be responsible. It just means that you live life looking for the joy, for the laughter, and for the fun. That's what makes life so much more enjoyable. It really is a conscious choice we make each day. Enjoy life and see the funny situations that surround us or make life a drudgery for yourself and everyone else around you. It's up to you. I hope you choose to Think BIG and Live Large with your Big Sense of Humor.

CHAPTER 10

Big Motivation

"I don't know how to motivate anybody. I just know that when a person has a genuine burning passion to do something, they'll give it all they have."

Are you motivated? Is everyone motivated? Yes. You and everyone around you is motivated in one way or another. Even someone frozen in place, not doing one single solitary thing, is motivated to do just that – absolutely nothing.

I don't know of many other words that have been as misunderstood or misused as much as the word motivation. Motivation is not what someone does or says to someone else. It is the stimulus that causes someone to think, say, or do anything.

To begin with, there are only two types of stimuli. One is external and the other is internal. A motivator is any kind of stimuli that causes a response to the stimuli. All external stimuli come in only two forms: Fear and Reward.

Internal stimuli are self-generated. It is what we call self talk, psyching ourselves up, giving ourselves a pep talk, or whatever else a person does to get themselves going. It can also be our response to an external stimulus. That response can be either positive or negative and can cause us to take some form of positive action, or it can illicit the "fight or flight" response that lives in each of us.

Let's take a look at fear from a leadership standpoint. As an external stimulator, does fear work? Yes, it works. My daddy proved that when I was just a boy. He'd leave the house in the summertime and on the way out, he'd look my way, smile and say, "Son, the grass is getting a little high." I usually picked up on his hint and would cut the grass before he got back home that night.

Sometimes, however, I would have other plans and wouldn't get around to cutting the grass. He would wait a day or two, to see if the first warning was enough. Then, he would be a little firmer as he went out the door and said, "You need to think about getting this grass cut soon." I would, of course say "Yes sir" and then go out and cut the grass. But on some occasions, I would, once again, have other plans. Maybe it was to go fishing, or to the river, or to build a tower with my friends, or better yet, cut a neighbors yard for <u>cash</u> money – never once seeing the value of the food, clothing and shelter I had at home.

In a day or two when <u>still</u> I had not cut the crass, he'd get down to motivating. Invariably, when the time came for him to do that, it would be early in the morning. He would be in the kitchen at one end of the house getting ready to leave, while I would be in the other end of the house back in my bedroom. He would holler very sternly for me, "Albert, I need to talk to you right now." Whenever he used those words, that way, that loud, I knew there was no danger of my going to him and hearing him say, "Oh, son. We love you." That voice inflection with those words meant, "Son, you are in trouble," and I would immediately go to him with my head hung down, because I knew he was serious.

I can see him right now. He'd grab me by the shoulders, look me right square in the eye, and say, "When I come home tonight, if the grass isn't cut, I'm gonna kill you." I am certain my dad would have never done that, but I know full well that he was capable of taking me within an inch of my life.

Was I motivated to cut the grass? You betcha. However, I would intentionally do things to sabotage the effort. I'd do things like not cutting around some corners, not edging the sidewalk, etc. And I would also "dog cuss" my daddy every step of the way. One time, I didn't put oil in the lawn mower, hoping it would break down and then I would get out of any more cutting for a while.

Not putting any oil in did cause the lawn mower to burn up one time, and I remember thinking I'd showed <u>him</u> a thing or two. When he got home, he saw the uncut grass, found me, and asked me why it wasn't finished. I told him the lawnmower had broken. We went to examine it, and the first thing he did was check the oil. He turned to me and asked if I had put any oil in it. I played dumb (which has always been easy for me to do) and said, "Oil?" in about three syllables, as in "Aw eee ul." And he drawled back, "That's right, AW EEE UL?" I tried to explain to him I didn't know about that. He shrugged his shoulders, and accused me of intentionally burning up the lawnmower. We then went to the hardware store in his pick-up truck, bought a new lawnmower, and on the way home he asked me if I was still cutting grass for different people in the neighborhood, and he named a few. I told him that I was and he said, "Great! I want you to keep doing that all year and bring me the money. You are going to buy this new lawnmower." So, I not only learned that fear can be a great motivator, I also learned that you shouldn't destroy the equipment, because they will buy more, and you'll pay for it one way or another. The stimulus was Daddy's threat to harm me if I didn't do what he told me. I had a choice – cut or not cut the grass. I made a choice that the aggravation of having to cut the grass was a better option than the pain and suffering I would go through, knowing I would <u>still</u> have to, eventually, cut the grass

Being intensely focused on a single goal can also be a wonderful stimulus - a real motivator. One year when I was about 16 years old, my dad decided his boys needed to know how to plow with a mule. He said if tough times hit, at least, you'll be able to grow your own food. He made this decision one spring, just in time for us to plant the annual garden, which was only about half an acre, but it seemed a lot larger when you were working in it.

Only problem with this plowing thing was the fact that we didn't own a mule. But our neighbor Mr. Swygert did and Daddy asked him if he could borrow his mule and everything that went with it (today we would call them "attachments", so he could teach his boys how to plow. When the big day came, Daddy, my brother Tim, and I all piled into Daddy's pick-up truck and headed over to see Mr. Swygert.

By road Mr. Swygert lived about 3 miles from us. But through the woods and across a couple of pastures it was probably about half that. When we got to Mr. Swygert's, he was waiting for us. We loaded up all the lines we would need and the plow. Then Daddy turned to me with, "Son, we need you to ride the mule back over to the garden spot. The shortest way is through the woods behind Mr. Swygert's, across Darr & Susie Frick's pasture to the dirt road that leads down to where we are going to 'put in' our garden."

Well, I got all excited about being the official mule rider. I had been around mules most of my life and they were all gentle creatures who were fun to ride. I hopped up on the mule's back and headed for the woods. There was a path down through the woods, but it wasn't much of one. Tree limbs hung down at various levels and the underbrush on each side of the path was thick and stuck out into the path a little. With the mule just plodding along, I had plenty of time to reach out for a limb and lift it up so I could get under it, or I could push the underbrush aside fairly easily. I finally came out of the woods into the bright sunshine and the Frick's pasture. I opened the gate, rode into the pasture just a few feet, got off the mule and closed the gate. I hopped back up on the mule and headed for the other side of the pasture, where I opened the other gate, rode through, and then closed it. Then I had to ride a couple of tenths of a mile down to the garden spot.

I remember us plowing all day. When we got through we were dusty and dirty, but before I could go for a swim in the nearby lake, I had to ride the mule back the same way I had come, and Daddy and Tim had to take all the equipment back to Mr. Swygert. The ole mule and I were both tired and we plodded our way back up the dirt road then into and, at last, out of Mr. Frick's pasture. The mule seemed barely able to put one hoof in front of the other as we went up the road and across the pasture.

HOWEVER, when we started up the path through the woods, the mule realized where we were headed. He laid his ears back, stuck his neck out, and took off like he was a Kentucky thoroughbred coming out of the starting gate at Churchill Downs, which by the way, is a gorgeous place. I recommend it highly. I digress. Anyway, as the mule flew up the path that led toward his barn and his food, all those limbs and underbrush I had been able to gently move out of my way earlier that day, were now slicing and dicing me to pieces. The limbs were about to knock me off the mule's back and the underbrush was cutting my legs up so badly that I thought I was going to bleed to death. All of a sudden we popped out of the woods back on Mr. Swygert's property. That's when it got worse. The mule spotted the barn and picked up speed. As he was about to run through the barn door, he started slowing down just a little. That is when I kind of half jumped and half fell off.

I was cut up from head to toe, filthy as could be, and now, to add insult to injury, I looked over where my Daddy and Mr. Swygert were standing, and they were both holding their sides, doubled over with laughter. I was mad as I could be. Of all things, how in the world could these two men be laughing at me. I was injured. I needed help. I jumped up and went and sat in the cab of the truck 'till Daddy could regain his composure and drive me home.

When he got in the cab, he explained to me what had happened. It seems that almost every mule will become super energized after working all day when they realize they are headed to their stall, where there is something to eat and drink and some clean hay to sleep on. In other words, when a mule gets refocused it gets reenergized. The minute that mule realized that everything he ever wanted was not far away and the sooner he got there, the sooner he could enjoy the peace, joy, and fulfillment anything or anyone feels when they get what they are going after. All of the obstacles in his way didn't matter: the couple of hundred pounds on his back (that was me), the bushes, limbs and stickers in his way, and the fact that he was dog tired were not going to keep him from his objective. The mule was focused.

That's what happens to us as well. The most lethargic times in my life have been when I've lost my focus. The most energized times have been when I was totally focused on one clear objective. The mule was motivated to action by the anticipation of a reward. Anticipation of the rewards of life motivates us humans.

Sharing this true story with you reminds me of another story on motivation I heard years ago. It seems a young boy of 9 or 10 years of age lived on a farm and had to walk to school every morning and walk back home every afternoon in time to get his chores done. He could see the school house from his back porch, but he couldn't walk directly to it, because it meant he would have to cross a huge pasture wherein lived one of the meanest bulls in the county. His parents told him to go around the pasture to get to school, so he followed the fence line all around the pasture twice a day.

One day, he stayed around school a little longer than he should have and realized that if he didn't get home in time to do his chores, he'd be in a heap of trouble. He knew if he went back home the usual way, around the fence line, he wouldn't get home until after dark and he wouldn't get his chores completed. That could cause him a lot of physical and emotional pain.

He decided he would try crossing the pasture. He could see his house from school and just knew it wouldn't be a problem. He got up close to the fence and looked everywhere for that old bull. He didn't see him anywhere, so he crawled through the barbed wire and backed up to the fence and looked again, just to be sure. He didn't see the bull anywhere. He took off running towards his house.

As he got to the middle of the pasture, all of a sudden the ground began to shake like it does when a train is coming. He glanced back over his shoulder and there he was. The biggest, meanest, snort'nest bull he had ever seen and the bull was closing the gap. The little guy picked up speed and began to run faster than he had ever run in his life, but the bull was closing in and getting closer and closer. It wasn't long before the boy could almost feel the hot air blowing out of the bull's pulsating nostrils. Out of the corner of his eye, the young boy spotted the lone tree that stood near the middle of the pasture. He decided to make a run for the tree. As he got closer and closer to the tree, he realized the first limb closest to the ground was still a good ten to twelve feet over his head. It didn't matter. He had to try and jump up to that limb. Just as the bull was about to run him down, the young man took a tremendous leap for the limb and he missed it. But he caught it on the way back <u>down!</u> The little guy was motivated.

Want to know what I do to get myself cranked up and motivated? I give myself a good talking too. Some have called it "self talk," which we are constantly engaged in when we aren't talking to someone else. Seems to me that if that is true, why not make it positive self talk as opposed to negative self talk.

Here is how it works.

First, I make sure I'm real clear about what I want to accomplish. Then I give myself a PEP talk. Yep, you read it right – a good ole fashioned PEP talk. It is a lot more than a rah rah speech I give myself. It is a structured self talk that really is - A Promise of Exceptional Performance talk and it consists of three parts. I mentioned it in the introduction at the front of the book.

Part one is a statement that I will accomplish the goal.
Part two consists of three or more reasons why I will accomplish my goal. Part Three lists at least three benefits that will come to me when I do accomplish it.

I don't focus on why I can't reach my goal, the obstacles in my way or the uncertainties that might exist. I focus on my strengths and what I will gain.

I also say a little prayer right before I go on. The words are straight out of the Bible and are in a song we've sung in my church choir. They are: "Let the words of my mouth and the meditations of my heart be acceptable in thy sight, oh, Lord, my strength and my redeemer." Now, thanks to our world class Minister of Music, Rev. Fred DeFoor having introduced us to the musical version, I now sing that little prayer to myself instead of just reciting it in my mind.

As I was writing this chapter I received another phone call from someone who wanted me to come speak to their people and get them motivated. I agreed to speak to his folks (in this case salespeople), but I told him not to be disappointed if some of them didn't get "turned on" and "charged up" by what I said. I told him that all I could do was try to create an inspiring climate and provide some thoughts that might stimulate their thinking about the importance of achieving their goals. If they agreed with me, then they just might be able to use what I said as a stimulus to motivate themselves later. I told him that I would challenge them to think not only about their goals, but also to think about the personal benefits they would enjoy if they did achieve their goals. The truth is, goal achievement by itself, doesn't motivate anybody. What motivates us is the anticipated reward we will receive for achieving or reaching our goal.

All of the great motivators know that what they do is just turn on the switch. Once they do, it's up to the light to keep shining. Find out what turns your switch on and your light will burn brighter. That's how you generate and maintain BIG Motivation.

CONCLUSION

The MO-SO theory says that whatever you are today, you will be more so of tomorrow. I don't know where I first heard about this. If I could remember who shared it with me, I would certainly give them credit. I just know I latched on to it and bought into it, hook, line, and sinker. The theory continues to prove itself time and time again.

My wife's mother, Louise Igleheart, dealt with Alzheimer's for about 8 years. Her last few years were spent at Martha Frank's Retirement Center, a fabulous, extremely well run facility in Laurens, South Carolina, that is operated by South Carolina Baptists.

One of the fascinating aspects of this insidious disease is that even when Alzheimer's patients can't tell you who <u>you</u> are, or who <u>they</u> are, they can remember the words to every song they ever learned. Go to an Alzheimer's unit this next Christmas and gather with them around a piano and join them, as they sing words to every Christmas Carol that is played – even words you have forgotten.

I had the privilege of meeting several very interesting people in that Alzheimer's unit and throughout the other areas of that facility. It was interesting that about half of the women who had been diagnosed with the disease, had been school teachers.

Mrs. Sallie Mae Meeks was a patient in the same area as Mrs. Louise. Margaret and I would visit with her sometimes and found out that Mrs. Sallie Mae loved to sing two particular songs. One was a song about the buffalo killings out west back in the late 1800's and the other was "You Are My Sunshine." As you know, the last line of the chorus is "Please don't take my sunshine away." Not for Mrs. Sallie Mae. She ended it every time with "Please don't take my <u>love life</u> away." I told my wife, I wish I had known her in her younger days. I bet she was a lot of fun. Mrs. Sallie Mae proved to me, once and for all, the validity of the MO - SO Theory. When she was in a state of mind where she couldn't tell you much about the world around her, she continued to have the spirit that she'd had probably all of her life. She was just more of what she had been, when she didn't have Alzheimer's.

I hope this book will enable you to clarify your values, laugh BIG, expect BIG things, maintain a high level of curiosity, dream BIG dreams, be able to persist in the tough times, be more authentic every day, give BIG doses of love, use your God given sense of humor in a BIG way, and that it has been the "turned on" switch you might have needed to go after the important things in life, so that you will be able to Think BIGGER and Live LARGER than you've ever thought and lived before.

INDEX

AL WALKER. . . . . . .A BIG MAN WITH A BIG MESSAGE

An emcee once asked his audience following one of Al's talks how many of them would like to take Al home. Most of them raised their hands, then one lone voice said, "as long as I don't have to feed him." Well, there is a way for anyone who wants to do so, to have Al in their home or in their vehicle to share his wit & wisdom with friends, family and co-workers. His video and audio programs and his books will enable you to do just that. They also make great gifts. Just photo copy this page and fax to (803) 345-1049 or mail to Al Walker – PO Box 542 – Chapin, SC 29036 OR go directly to www.alwalker.com and place your order on-line

Video Tapes or DVD	Quantity	Cost
The Gateway to Excellence is as Big as a Barn		29.95
Thinking Big and Living Large		29.95
Audio Cassette or CD		
A World Fit To Live In		9.95
Books		
Thinking Big and Living Large		14.95
Standing on The Threshold of Greatness		17.95
Total		
Shipping and Handling		6.00
SC residents add sales tax		
Check or credit card total		

For Credit Card Orders: ❑ MC   ❑ Visa   ❑ Amex   ❑ Discover

Card #: _____ Exp. Date: _____

Signature: _____

Ship to:

Name:_____

Address: _____ Suite or Apt.#_____

City: _____ State: ____ Zip: _____

Phone: (____)_____ email: _____

FOR YOUR NEXT PROGRAM

WHY NOT CHOOSE

AL WALKER LIVE & IN PERSON?

For information regarding Al's program titles, availability, fees, and other information contact us at 1-(800) 255-1982 or you may email us at info@alwalker.com. Visit us on the web at www.alwalker.com.

Keynote, Luncheon and After Dinner topics include:

A WORLD FIT TO LIVE IN

Through humorous anecdotes and stories, AL delivers the driving message that in order for us to have a world fit to live in, we must first have a self worth living with and a philosophy to live by. AL defines exactly what it takes to have a "self worth living with" and knows how knowledge, skill and attitude contribute to that goal.

THE GATEWAY TO EXCELLENCE IS AS BIG AS A BARN

It's true – the path may be narrow but the gateway is huge and yet so few choose to walk through it. Instead, they settle for mediocrity not realizing that the difference between excellence and average is not vast or striking. In an entertaining and inspiring fashion, AL shares the secrets to the small characteristics that make the **BIG** differences in anyone's quest for excellence. Your audience will laugh, cry and go away feeling like a million dollars with a smile on their faces and in their hearts.

TRAINING & DEVELOPMENT PROGRAMS

Al Walker & Associates, Inc. provides workshops, break out sessions, and on-going training in such topics as:

Sales, sales management, leadership, customer service, teambuilding, change management, time management, speaking skills, project management, business planning and personal development skills.